AF574936

AMERICAN PAINTINGS IN SOUTHERN CALIFORNIA COLLECTIONS

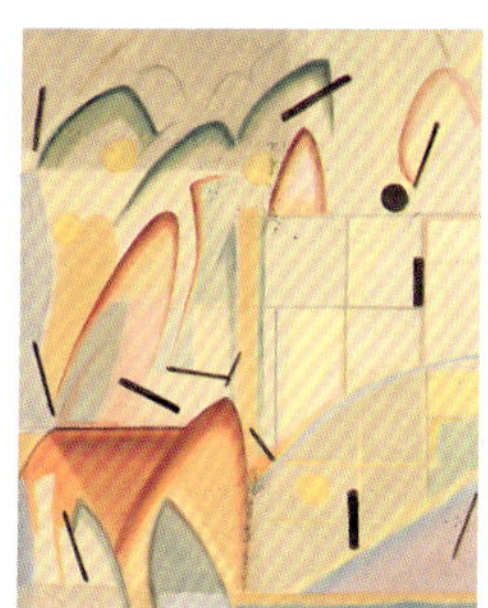

AMERICAN PAINTINGS IN

Southern California Collections

From Gilbert Stuart to Georgia O'Keeffe

Ilene Susan Fort

with Trudi Abram

Los Angeles County Museum of Art

AMERICAN PAINTINGS IN
SOUTHERN CALIFORNIA COLLECTIONS
From Gilbert Stuart to Georgia O'Keeffe

Los Angeles County Museum of Art
March 17–May 26, 1996

THIS EXHIBITION WAS ORGANIZED BY THE
LOS ANGELES COUNTY MUSEUM OF ART
AND WAS SUPPORTED BY GRANTS FROM THE
WILLAMETTA K. DAY FOUNDATION AND
CECILE BARTMAN.

SUPPORT FOR
THE EXHIBITION CATALOGUE
WAS PROVIDED BY
ABBY AND ALAN D. LEVY,
CAROLE AND TED SLAVIN, AND
BENTE AND GERALD E. BUCK.

Published by the
Los Angeles County Museum of Art
5905 Wilshire Boulevard,
Los Angeles, California 90036

Edited by Thomas Frick
Designed by Amy McFarland
Photography by Jay McNally

This book was typeset in Stempel Garamond and printed by Hull Printing Co., Meriden, Connecticut.

Cover:
THOMAS MORAN
The Green River, Wyoming, 1879,
(detail)

Half-title and title pages:
MANIERRE DAWSON
Prognostic, 1910,
(detail)

Photo credits:
COURTESY GUGGENHEIM, ASHER ASSOCIATES INC.:
Childe Hassam, *Champs Elysées, Paris*
Jared French, *Chess and Politics*
Frederic Remington, *Attack on the Supply Wagons*

COURTESY JORDAN-VOLPE GALLERY, NEW YORK:
James A.M. Whistler, *Portrait of Ellen Sturgis Hooper*

LARRY REYNOLDS:
Dwight Tryon, *Early Morning (Dawn–Early Spring)*

JOSEPH COSCIA JR., NEW YORK:
Stanton MacDonald-Wright,
Synchromy (possibly *Portrait of Artist*)

All other paintings reproduced courtesy of the lenders

LIBRARY OF CONGRESS CATALOGUE NUMBER:
95-081976

ISBN: 0-87587-175-5

Contents

President's Foreword

AMERICAN PAINTINGS IN SOUTHERN CALIFORNIA COLLECTIONS: FROM GILBERT STUART TO GEORGIA O'KEEFFE presents the development of American painting over a century and a half, from eighteenth-century Federal portraiture to mid-twentieth-century abstraction. In so doing, it reveals the acumen of collectors in Southern California, who have had the foresight and taste to acquire wisely. They have revealed no preference for a single aesthetic or movement but instead have demonstrated the eclecticism that has long characterized our region. There are many marvelous paintings hidden away in private homes; the present display is a sampling.

This is actually the second exhibition devoted to the local taste for American painting. Twenty-two years ago the museum heralded the new popularity of our country's heritage with *American Paintings from Los Angeles Collections*. As the present exhibition demonstrates, American art has continued to increase in popularity. *American Paintings in Southern California Collections: From Gilbert Stuart to Georgia O'Keeffe* is also the second LACMA exhibition in five years devoted to the artistic treasures of our larger community. In 1991 the museum offered *Monet to Matisse: French Art in Southern California Collections*, which not only demonstrated the popularity of modern French art but also the significance of the region's private holdings. This exhibition fulfills a similar purpose.

The real pleasure in organizing an exhibition such as this one is the opportunity it gives the museum's staff to acquaint and reacquaint ourselves with so many devoted collectors and art lovers in the region. Without their overwhelming enthusiasm and cooperation such an undertaking could not have been realized. We express our gratitude to the lenders, who enthusiastically agreed to share their paintings with the Southern California audience, as well as to the many other collectors who opened their homes to us.

The museum would like to thank the Willametta K. Day Foundation and Cecile Bartman for generously funding the exhibition. Additional support for the exhibition catalogue was provided by Abby and Alan D. Levy, Carole and Ted Slavin, and Bente and Gerald E. Buck. We appreciate patronage of this sort for it clearly demonstrates the region's passion for American art.

We would also like to express our appreciation to those staff members and friends of the museum who tracked the locations of paintings and assisted in bringing them to the galleries. We would especially like to acknowledge the efforts of Ilene Susan Fort, curator of American art, who organized the exhibition and wrote the catalogue essay on the history of Southern California collecting, and Trudi Abram, who provided the contextual introductions to the five thematic sections.

American Paintings in Southern California Collections: From Gilbert Stuart to Georgia O'Keeffe clearly demonstrates our region's important role in collecting American art. We hope that visitors to the exhibition will experience a sense of pride as well as enjoyment.

Andrea L. Rich
President and CEO

Collecting American Art in Southern

"Within the last few years the advance of public Taste and the increased recognition of art in this country, have been among the most interesting phenomena of the times.... Private collections of pictures have become a new social attraction."

Henry T. Tuckerman (1867)[1]

California ❧

IT HAS OFTEN been claimed that Southern California has few significant collectors of American art because the region has no tradition of collecting. Both the premise and the conclusion of this statement are false; there have been important collectors in the region for over three-quarters of a century.[2]

During the first decades of this century Southern California resonated with the same ambition experienced by the burgeoning nation in the early 1800s—the desire to demonstrate its importance and sophistication through the establishment of culture.[3] Collecting is part of the history of culture and as such is closely tied to the growth of cities and general economic development. The southern expanse of California did not experience urbanization until the present century, long after cities had arisen along the eastern seaboard, throughout the Midwest, and in the northern part of the state. Boosterism was rampant, as promoters extolled the virtues of the new Garden of Eden to the people back East: warm weather, wide-open spaces, and a spirit of freedom beckoned new settlers. Civic-minded residents did realize that if the area were to compete with the East it had to display some signs of culture by supporting libraries, museums, symphonies, and theaters, institutions that would instruct the public's taste.

It was natural that Los Angeles, the largest urban center in the region, should establish the first art museum and be the home of the first significant collector; the city would retain its leadership in the arts throughout the century. The Los Angeles Museum of History, Science, and Art (part of which became the Los Angeles County Museum of Art in 1965) was founded in 1910 and opened in 1913. In 1915 the Friends of American Art group was formed under the auspices of the California Art Club to secure funds for purchasing works for the museum's permanent collection.[4] The first painting

1. Henry T. Tuckerman, *Book of the Artists: American Artist Life*, 2nd ed. (New York: G. P. Putnam & Son, 1867), 11.

2. The full history of collecting in Southern California is yet to be written. This modest essay is offered only as an introduction to the topic. Because of its brevity, not all of the many collectors who have been active in the region could be mentioned.

3. The premise of Russell Lynes' seminal book *The Tastemakers* is that a constant theme in our country's history has been, "If America is to be great, America must have culture." (New York: Grosset & Dunlap, 1954), 7.

4. "Los Angeles," *American Art News* 13 (May 1, 1915): 7

bought by the municipality forecast the dominance of American art in the region, for George Bellows' *Cliff Dwellers*, perhaps the museum's best-known painting by a twentieth-century American artist, was purchased in 1916, only three years after the museum's first building opened. Soon after, the region's pioneer collector of American art appeared on the scene.[5]

The son and brother of Chicago mayors, William Preston Harrison began visiting Southern California during the first decade of the century and with his wife, Ada, settled permanently in Los Angeles at the end of World War I. Harrison had already started collecting before his move west, acquiring contemporary paintings, often by artists with midwestern connections. Having earlier collected books, which he donated to the Huntington Library in San Marino, he became obsessed with the desire to be the benefactor of a significant museum art collection. In 1918 the Harrisons began their philanthropic contributions to the fledgling Los Angeles Museum and explained their rationale in a letter to its director, Frank S. Daggett:

> It is with more than ordinary delight and satisfaction that we would make this gift to the people of Los Angeles County —and we hope earnestly and sincerely thereby to stimulate in this community an increased interest in Art and that this collection of ours will become the nucleus of a really magnificent Art Gallery...that perhaps many public-minded residents will follow the example.[6]

Through their collection the Harrisons hoped to demonstrate that Los Angeles was no longer a provincial town.

The twenty-eight paintings they donated in 1918 were largely by American impressionist, ashcan, and southwestern artists. Harrison eventually made a legal agreement to continue his donations as long as two stipulations would be met: that the collection be housed in a room known as the Harrison

5. There were a few residents who collected art prior to this time, but their purchasing and patronage had no consistency. See passing references in Nancy Dustin Wall Moure's *Loners, Mavericks & Dreamers: Art in Los Angeles Before 1900*. Exh. cat. Laguna Art Museum, 1993.

6. Harrison to Daggett, February 25, 1918, LACMA archives; reprinted in Harrison 1918, n.p.

Gallery, and that he be able to change the paintings at any time, a process of upgrading he deemed essential to achieve a quality collection. Consequently the Harrison Gallery was not a static entity. Harrison traveled frequently to Chicago, New York, and abroad in his pursuit of important paintings. Not trusting dealers, he preferred to buy directly from the artists. Harrison continued to focus on contemporary art, digressing only occasionally to purchase works by such esteemed painters as Thomas Eakins, Henry O. Tanner, and Elihu Vedder. He soon abandoned his early interest in Taos-based painters to concentrate primarily on artists who lived and exhibited in the East. To ensure a high standard for his purchases he sought out those artists who were academicians or had won official recognition in the form of prizes, and he compared his selections with the holdings of the Metropolitan Museum of Art, the Art Institute of Chicago, and other similarly prestigious older institutions. He preferred conservative figure painters such as John Costigan, Arthur B. Davies, Guy Pène du Bois, and Leopold Seyffert; Childe Hassam was his favorite. In the late 1920s Harrison turned to American watercolors and in this new medium became more daring, selecting modernist works by Charles Demuth, Preston Dickinson, and William Zorach. Most of his American collection was given to the museum by the mid-1930s, and for his generosity Harrison was appointed to the board of governors and made an honorary curator of art.

Soon after the Harrisons appeared, another equally far-sighted person, whose beneficence would be crucial to the development of two other museums, began collecting. Josephine Everett, widow of Cleveland telephone and electrical-railway magnate Henry A. Everett, began wintering in California in 1912. Starting in 1919 her Pasadena home became the site of many cultural events and was kept open so that local residents could enjoy her art collection. She, like Harrison, was both patron and collector, for she too preferred to buy directly from the artists. She believed in supporting American talent, especially the young, as a means of ensuring America's future as a world cultural leader. Although Everett was considered during her life one of the country's foremost sponsors of American artists, her patronage has since been overshadowed by her East Coast counterparts. The scope of her acquiring was comparable to the Harrisons'.

It is not known when she began purchasing American art, but in 1927 an exhibition of seventy-five paintings from her collection went on view at the new Fine Arts Gallery of San Diego. (Founded the year before, it was the forerunner of the San Diego Museum of Art.) She initiated the practice of annual Christmas gifts to that institution with the donation of a coastal scene by John Twachtman and an art deco bronze by C. Paul Jennewein. Everett soon became a close friend of Reginald Poland, the gallery's director, and an honorary vice president of the museum. At her death in 1937 her collection was divided among the San Diego Museum, the Pasadena Art Museum (which had opened its doors in 1924 as the Pasadena Art Institute), and the Cleveland Museum of Art.[7] Her generous gifts—including works by George Bellows, Mary Cassatt, George Inness, Luigi Lucioni, and Willard Metcalf—formed the basis for the American painting collection at the Fine Arts Gallery of San Diego in much the same way that the Harrisons' bequests formed the nucleus of the Los Angeles Museum's collection. Pasadena received works by such renowned artists as Ralph A. Blakelock, William M. Chase, Frederick Frieseke, and Jerome Myers. Unfortunately these were dispersed at auction

7. Unlike Harrison Everett never lived in California the year round; her allegiance was split between Southern California and Cleveland. The dispersion of her art collection reflected her continued support of the Cleveland Museum of Art.

after the institution became the Norton Simon Museum and revised its collecting mandate.

Like some of the most famous early-nineteenth-century American collectors, Harrison and Everett made most of their purchases from living artists and enjoyed interacting with them. Although art collectors had been rare in colonial times, by the first decades of the nineteenth century progressive Americans realized the need to rectify the country's lack of artistic cultivation. Thomas H. Perkins of Boston and Robert Gilmor Jr. of Baltimore were the first to collect contemporary American art in their respective cities. In the 1830s Luman Reed in New York furthered the cause of American painting not only by patronizing young artists such as Thomas Cole and Asher B. Durand of the Hudson River school but by creating a special gallery in his home to exhibit their works.[8] Reed hoped that his collection would form the basis of a public museum, and after his death it did become the core of the New-York Historical Society.

Harrison and Everett believed that the role of a collector went far beyond personal enjoyment, for both bought paintings with the foresight that they would ultimately reside in public institutions. They understood that a museum's prestige would be based on its permanent collection, which could only be realized through the efforts of private citizens. Harrison was realistic about his role:

> It is too tremendous a task to expect just one collector to cover so extended a field.... Nothing is quite so difficult to evaluate as art; doubly trying when it comes to contemporary or living art.... Any curator or collector when striving to perform a public deed or in usurping that privilege necessarily subjects himself to criticism and must accept the responsibility without a whimper.[9]

8. For a detailed discussion of early collecting and patronage in the United States see the essays by Wayne Craven and Ella M. Foshay in Foshay's *Mr. Luman Reed's Picture Gallery: A Pioneer Collection of American Art.* Exh. cat. New York: Harry N. Abrams in association with the New-York Historical Society, 1990.

9. Harrison quoted by Larry Curry in Harrison 1969, n.p.

Few others in the region during the pre–World War II era collected American art so consistently. Paul Rodman Mabury shared Harrison's boosterism, in that he hoped his art bequest would not only be enjoyed by the public but would contribute to the Los Angeles Museum's reputation. Yet his taste was catholic: his modest collection included outstanding nineteenth-century American paintings such as a Winslow Homer watercolor and an Albert Pinkham Ryder oil, but the focus was on European old masters. Such eclecticism was also characteristic of Mr. and Mrs. Allan Balch and other early collectors, all wealthy individuals of broad education and sophistication.

This personal taste for mixing European old masters and twentieth-century paintings—with only an occasional American art purchase—came to typify many of the region's most significant collectors well into the 1970s. In Santa Barbara Ala Story and Margaret Mallory began such a collection in the 1950s. But it was Wright Ludington who amassed perhaps the premiere holdings of this type. A founder of the Santa Barbara Museum of Art and one of its most generous patrons, Ludington purchased European, Asian, and some American art from the 1920s until his death in 1992.

The few Southern Californians who specialized in American art immediately after the war usually bought contemporary works, as had Harrison and Everett. However, this period also witnessed the emergence and growth of a new kind of collector, one who focused on historical art. (In fact, to collect "American art" has come to mean to buy American paintings and sculpture created prior to 1945; those who purchase more recent works are known simply as modern- or contemporary-art collectors.) The interest in older works arose in response to the general recognition of American art as a valid field of art history. From this time onward the taste of Southern California collectors, like that of their East Coast counterparts, would largely echo developments in American art history. Collectors would acquire works by artists esteemed by scholars and museums and available through commercial dealers.

Inspired partly by the federal art projects of the Depression, which promoted the idea of creating a democratic art accessible to the general public, historians looked back to an earlier expression of nativism. One hundred years before, writers, ministers, and politicians had extolled the importance of creating a truly national art. American artists of the mid-nineteenth century rose to the challenge by capturing the beauty of the American wilderness in landscape paintings and the pleasant life of ordinary American folk in genre scenes. Consequently there appeared during the 1930s and 1940s books and exhibitions examining colonial portraiture and the Hudson River school of landscape painting (such as the Metropolitan Museum of Art's groundbreaking 1939 *Life in America* show), and monographic studies of leading figures such as John Singleton Copley, Thomas Eakins, and Winslow Homer.

Although some scholars were fascinated by the biographies of the persons depicted in colonial art, few collectors in Southern California shared their interest in such portraiture. (This was the one exception to the tendency for collectors to follow trends in art scholarship.) Collecting in the 1930s, Mary and Fred Keeler of Los Angeles may have been the first to acquire portraits attributed to Gilbert Stuart. A few years ago Sandra and Jacob Terner donated to the Los Angeles County Museum of Art Copley's depiction of Bostonian Joseph Scott. Armand Hammer's best American paintings were portraits. The few other portraits in the region have usually not been bought by collectors, but have been family heirlooms passed down from one generation to another, and are only in this area because the family moved here. The sitters and owners of James Peale's handsome head of Samuel Allen and Chester Harding's charming depiction of Mrs. Nathaniel Willis represent families with long and notable ties to American history. A number of these family portraits have been donated to local museums, especially the San Diego Museum, during the past few decades.

Southern Californians who began purchasing historical American art in the decades after World War II usually focused on the nineteenth century and landscape painting. There was a precedent in the figure of Maxim Karolik of Rhode Island, the pioneer collector in this field, who in the late 1930s and early 1940s had amassed and given to the Museum of Fine Arts in Boston a huge collection of nineteenth-century landscape and genre paintings. George F. McMurray, and Vincent Newton and Joseph Holland, may have been the first in this region to concentrate on the Hudson River school. Later McMurray acquired Western landscapes. Although Oklahoman Thomas Gilcrease had been the most serious collector of Western art prior to World War II and had opened his own museum in 1949, by the 1950s a group of Southern Californians had emerged who also focused on the West and sometimes even narrowed their specialty to California. Their place of residence no doubt encouraged this fascination. The American West had long inspired romantics, and in the twentieth century it was given new mythic form on a popular level by the motion picture industry. The Western film was flourishing by 1915, and the greatest cinematic portrayer of Western history, John Ford, produced legendary examples in the 1940s. Californians who had grown up near studio locations with their fabricated frontier towns populated by actors in "cowboy and Indian" costumes responded to the familiarity of similar images in Western paintings.

The strong historical interests of these collectors often led them beyond the fine arts to include Western Americana in their holdings. Robert B. Honeyman bought topographical views, maps, letters, and printed ephemera, building the largest collection of Californiana in the world. Carl S. Dentzel, director of the Southwest Museum in Los Angeles from 1956 until his death in 1980, documented the introduction and expansion of European civilization in the West. His fascination with Native Americans and their culture spurred him to collect textiles, ceramics, and baskets in addition to paintings depicting their lives and customs. Because of his ethnographic approach and professional associations, Dentzel willed that his huge collection be distributed among the Southwest Museum, Phoenix Art Museum, Laguna Art Museum, and his family.

Earl Adams astutely realized the aesthetic quality as well as the historical importance of the paintings and sculptures of Edward Borein, Carl Oscar Borg, and Charles M. Russell. Elaine and Samuel Rosenthal acquired Western Americana because of Sam's fond memories of his youth in Montana. In 1969 Rose and Edward Boseker, recent transplants from Indiana, determined to collect images of their new home. They bought some of the earliest genre scenes by William Hahn and Thomas Ross in addition to the typical vistas of Yosemite and the Sierras by Thomas Hill and William Keith. Katherine Haley focused on the art of Edward Borein, while Frank Hathaway amassed a first-rate collection of works by Taos painters for the Los Angeles Athletic Club. By the 1980s some of the finest Western art holdings in private hands would reside in Southern California.

Other new collectors emerged in the 1960s, a period of economic prosperity engendered in large part by the booming aerospace industry. They realized that historical American painting was a relatively untouched as well as modestly priced field. This increasing acknowledgment was fostered by several events. Winslow Homer's quintessential epic scene, *Lost on the Grand Banks* (see p. 19), was removed from the National Gallery of Art, where it was on loan, and placed on view at the Los Angeles Museum because the owner, a Californian, wanted the painting closer to his home so that he could periodically visit it. Realizing its importance as one of Homer's finest seascapes and one of the last of the major paintings in private hands, he has generously continued his loan—now to LACMA—for the past four decades.[10]

Noted historian E. Maurice Bloch, himself a collector of American drawings, began teaching classes on American art in 1956 at the University of California, Los Angeles, thereby encouraging future generations of West Coast–based professionals in the field. In 1959 Terry De Lapp opened the first gallery in the West dedicated solely to American art. Two years later the Preston Morton collection was installed at the Santa Barbara Museum of Art, which had been devoted to American art since its opening in 1941. Morton had bought forty-six paintings with the advice of museum director James W. Foster Jr. for the express purpose of donating them to the institution. With the gift Santa Barbara became the first Southern California city to have on display a large historical survey of American painting. In 1965 the Los Angeles County Museum of Art, which had separated from its parent institution that year, established an American art department and named Larry Curry its first curator. Curry's classes in American art during 1968 and 1969, part of the UCLA extension program, gave birth to a generation of educated collectors.

The historian-collector of the early postwar era was to be replaced by the connoisseur-collector. Curry's classes were held at the home of Jo Ann and Julian Ganz Jr. The Ganzes had started acquiring American art in 1964; their

10. The painting was unavailable for this exhibition because it had previously been promised to the Winslow Homer retrospective organized by the National Gallery of Art.

WINSLOW HOMER
(1836–1910)
Lost on the Grand Banks, 1885
oil on canvas
30½ x 49⅜ in
(77.5 x 126 cm)
anonymous loan to the
Los Angeles County Museum of Art

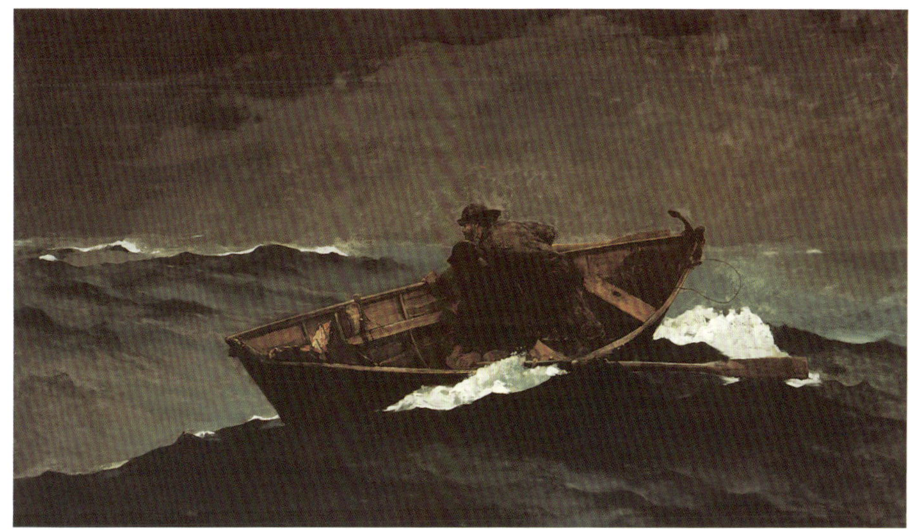

initial purchase was a painting by Robert Henri. By the time of the first public showing of their collection, in 1969 at the Los Angeles County Museum of Art, they had expanded their holdings to include turn-of-the-century impressionists as well as the New York–based group the Eight. At that time Curry praised them for not following the tendency to see American art "as a sociological manifestation rather than as a form of creative expression."[11] With them, Southern California collectors of American art had finally rejected artifacts for the fine arts. Quality now became the major criterion. Over the next three decades the Ganzes modified and refined their tastes, changing the focus of their collection until they had amassed the most significant private holdings of American art in Southern California as well as one of the finest in the country. Their paintings include still lifes, trompe l'oeil compositions, genre scenes, and landscapes by Albert Bierstadt, Frederic Church, William Harnett,

11. Curry in Ganz 1969, n.p.

Martin Johnson Heade, Winslow Homer, Eastman Johnson, Raphaelle Peale, and John F. Peto. Over the decades the Ganzes have also supported and donated to LACMA. Their exquisite taste in exactitude and realism, love of truly American imagery, and focus on the nineteenth century would become the gauge by which other collections were measured. Elma and Charles Shoemaker followed the Ganzes' lead by building an important collection of mid-nineteenth-century paintings, and in 1994 bequeathing it to the Los Angeles County Museum of Art and the Santa Barbara Museum.

Other developments encouraged the spread of interest in historical American painting. In 1971 the Friends of American Art was organized by the Ganzes with the assistance of Patricia Gilfillan; two years later it became the American Art Council. The council was, and still is, the major support group of the American art department of the Los Angeles County Museum of Art. One of its primary aims is education, and its activities have inspired many new collectors. Also in 1971 Sotheby Parke Bernet opened a branch office in Los Angeles and within a few years held lectures and auctions devoted to American art, thereby assisting collectors who did not have the time to visit New York. Two years later the bimonthly *American Art Review* began publishing in Los Angeles. By 1974 there were enough quality paintings in private hands in the city to hold a special exhibition, *American Paintings from Los Angeles Collections*, at LACMA. The exhibition was organized by Donelson Hoopes, who had succeeded Larry Curry as curator in 1972 and who would play an important role in the early growth of the council, encouraging it to support major purchases for the museum. Seventy-four paintings from thirty-two collections spanned the years from 1818 through the 1950s. Although two generations of collectors were represented, Western art was not emphasized;

instead, nineteenth-century East Coast imagery dominated and would continue to do so for the next decade.

During the past two decades interest in American art has intensified to a degree never before witnessed in the region. Patronage of the arts has long been identified in the minds of Americans with successful merchants, manufacturers, and financiers. With the land boom and the strong aerospace industry of the early 1980s, Southern California experienced another period of economic prosperity, and a new group of collectors arose, many with fortunes based in real estate. The Bicentennial, with all its celebrations and numerous publications, popularized American art throughout the country. In 1979 Frederic Church's *The Iceberg* attracted national attention when it became the first American painting to bring more than a million dollars in a public auction. Also in 1979 the Virginia Steele Scott Foundation agreed to establish and maintain an American art collection at the Huntington Library and Art Gallery in San Marino, and five years later it opened to the public. The Smithsonian Institution's Archives of American Art opened a branch in Southern California, also at the Huntington, in 1984.

The Bicentennial caused scholars to reassess the era of the Centennial, a time when American culture entered the international arena and grew more cosmopolitan in character. Victorian art of the mid-nineteenth century was still popular, but impressionism, academic salon painting, and urban realism began to attract collectors, especially from the younger generation. Although American impressionist works would escalate in price by the late 1980s—when Frederick Frieseke's *The Open Window* brought $750,000, a Childe Hassam flag painting $2.9 million, and a Mary Cassatt pastel $4.1 million—they were still more affordable than European examples. Academic painting was tempting both in its technical beauty and modest price. Michael Quick, curator of American art from 1976 to 1993 at the Los Angeles County Museum of Art and a specialist in late-nineteenth-century painting, encouraged local collectors. Some followed his advice to narrow their focus and amassed holdings devoted to academic figure painting, American orientalism, the Aesthetic Movement and tonalism (often this taste was combined with the collecting of Asian arts), the Eight, or the ashcan school. Many other collectors, however, continued to prefer a wider range of themes and styles, though usually still limited to the turn-of-the-century period.

Interest in American modernism has always been a minor voice. In the early part of the century no Southern California patron comparable to John Quinn in New York and Ferdinand Howald in Columbus, Ohio, concentrated solely on the American avant-garde. As an art student in New York during the 1920s Wright Ludington became friends with Charles Demuth, John Marin, and other progressive artists and discovered Alfred Stieglitz's gallery An American Place; consequently he bought exquisite pastels and watercolors by first-generation American modernists. However, the failure of the Modern Institute of Art in Beverly Hills and the loss of the Arensberg collection from the region did not bode well for progressive art in general.

During the autumn of 1947 a group of enthusiastic art collectors, including Vincent Price and Fanny Brice, organized the Modern Institute of Art, the first museum in the area devoted solely to modern trends, in the hope of eventually inducing Walter Arensberg to donate his collection. Although it held many landmark exhibitions and had a large membership, the institution never received the necessary financial backing from wealthy Angelenos and was forced to close in 1949.

Walter C. and Louise Arensberg had settled in Hollywood in 1921, bringing with them a renowned collection of twentieth-century avant-garde art, primarily European; they continued to add to their holdings with purchases from the local gallery founded by Earl Stendahl in 1927. During the 1930s and 1940s the Arensbergs attempted to place their collection with a suitable West Coast institution. The Los Angeles Museum demonstrated no interest—its trustees thought Arensberg too progressive—and the University of California regents failed to find a suitable building to house the works. With the closing of the Modern Institute of Art, the Arensbergs looked beyond the region, ultimately giving their collection to the Philadelphia Museum of Art in 1950.

The Arensbergs' example did encourage a few others, such as Ruth Maitland, to purchase American works along with European modernist masterpieces. The Arensbergs and Maitland patronized a number of the most progressive artists working in the area, among them Stanton Macdonald-Wright, Helen Lundeberg, and Elise (Elise Cavanna Seeds Armitage). From the late 1950s to the 1970s Earle Grant and Pliny Munger in La Jolla gathered an eclectic grouping of modern masterpieces with the assistance of Dalzell Hatfield, the most important Los Angeles dealer in modern art at the time. Settling in La Jolla in the 1960s Barbara and Norton Walbridge became significant figures in the modern and contemporary art scene, purchasing works by Georgia O'Keeffe, Joseph Stella, and Stuart Davis; their donations to the San Diego Museum formed the basis of the institution's American modernist holdings.

Collecting historical American modernism is a recent development, and only in the past decade have there appeared a few collections specializing in native avant-gardism. Most are focused on the first generation of modernists, those artists associated with the New York dealers Alfred Stieglitz and Charles Daniel. Peter Fischer is the exception, for he is concerned with a later generation—New York artists associated with the American Abstract Artists group.

Preferring the clean edge and precision of the geometric abstractionists of the 1930s and 1940s, Fischer daringly bought works by George L. K. Morris, John Ferren, and Harry Holtzman, artists long overshadowed by the abstract expressionists. He started in this field when it was still virgin territory and today his historical modernist collection is one of the finest in the country and certainly unique in California. Fannie and Alan Leslie of Palm Springs have also followed their personal taste for the later phase of modernism, their earliest paintings dating from the 1930s. Although they have works by Will Henry Stevens, a teacher of Fannie's, they focus primarily on California and Southwest movements as evidenced in the work of surrealists Ben Berlin and Charles Howard, and transcendentalists Raymond Jonson and Ed Garman; many of these they have generously promised to the Los Angeles County Museum of Art.

Interest in American Scene painting of the 1930s also developed late. These representational depictions of contemporary life included the heroic images of the regionalists as well as critical attacks on the injustices of the Depression by the social realists. Social realism especially appeals to a number of collectors who came of age in the 1960s and experienced the turbulent era of the Vietnam War. The mass-media quality of the American Scene aesthetic, with its emphasis on the common man, has also attracted people involved in the entertainment industry. Film is essentially a visual medium, and so it is logical that a passion for art has a long history among actors, directors, and producers. During the 1930s and 1940s Charles Laughton, Vincent Price, and Edward G. Robinson were among the most active and visible collectors of the Southern California art scene, but they focused largely on impressionist and modernist Europeans and contemporary artists. Not until American painting achieved some status in the history of world art did Hollywood begin to pay attention.

An overriding characteristic among the younger generation has been its interest in art with a strong narrative component. This may suggest the pervasive influence of film and television, which are overwhelmingly involved in presenting stories. From 1970 until his death in 1992 television writer Ken Trevey collected Depression-period prints. Because of their modest cost, availability, and thematic concern with common folk, these prints are an art form, like motion pictures, that has widespread appeal. Paintings with similarly populist imagery by Thomas Hart Benton, Jared French, Edward Hopper, and Norman Rockwell have been enthusiastically collected by others in the entertainment industry.

The new interest in regionalism further encouraged collectors in different areas of the country to examine their local artistic heritages. Previously the region's few serious collectors of American art had shared William Preston Harrison's opinion: "[I]t is not California art nor Chicago art nor New York art that spells anything in particular. It is open competition where all sections are represented."[12] It was a fear of being considered provincial that for decades prevented collectors in Southern California from amassing serious holdings of their state's early art. California art should have achieved esteem along with the popularity of Western art in general, but it did not.

Although the Oakland Museum decided to specialize in (and thereby officially sanction) California themes in 1961, it was a single person, curator Nancy Moure, who in the 1970s gave the region's art respectability through her scholarly documentation of Southern California's artistic production.[13] Around 1973 she and her husband, Joseph, began unearthing long-forgotten impressionist paintings. By the 1980s, collecting California plein-air painting, as such work became known, had become fashionable. Even though the sun-

12. Harrison to William A. Bryan, director of the Los Angeles Museum, December 7, 1921. Harrison correspondence, registrar archives, LACMA, and LACMA papers, Archives of American Art.

13. For example, Nancy Dustin Wall Moure, *The California Water Color Society: Prize Winners, 1931–1954; Index to Exhibitions, 1921–1954*. Publications in Southern California Art, no. 1 (Los Angeles: privately printed, 1973); and Moure and Phyllis Moure, *Artists' Clubs and Exhibitions in Los Angeles before 1930*. Publications in Southern California Art, no. 2 (Los Angeles: privately printed, 1975).

drenched landscapes suited the casual lifestyles of many new collectors and the modern designs of their homes, the taste in Southern California painting was triggered in part by the escalating prices in American impressionism generally. Commercial galleries devoted solely to California art sprang up throughout the state; the largest West Coast auctioneer, Butterfield and Butterfield, initiated "all California" sales in 1985; and even older, established East Coast galleries began selling early California impressionist paintings. In 1992 the Irvine Museum was founded. Inspired by love of her native state, especially its unique natural environment, Joan Irvine Smith went beyond merely collecting California paintings for her own enjoyment to create a public arena where generations to come could learn about and enjoy the history and beauty of California.

Seldom did collectors of California painting depart from charming impressionist landscapes to purchase the somber realist scenes of California life in the 1930s or the first expressions of the avant-garde. A few renegades bought 1930s and 1940s watercolors of California scenes, or modernist oils. However, the most adventuresome collectors were Bente and Gerald Buck. Beginning in 1984 they acquired some of the most important examples of avant-garde art, paintings by Elise, Lorser Feitelson, Helen Lundeberg, and Agnes Pelton. In the tradition of Joseph Hirshhorn, the Bucks often bought multiple works of an artist, so that they built not only the largest private collection of twentieth-century California art but also in-depth holdings of some of the region's pioneer progressives.

Today we celebrate the present state of American art in Southern California by this exhibition of seventy-nine exceptional paintings. Collecting is a private activity, but such ownership carries with it certain public responsi-

13. For example, Nancy Dustin Wall Moure, *The California Water Color Society: Prize Winners, 1931-1954; Index to Exhibitions, 1921-1954.* Publications in Southern California Art, no. 1 (Los Angeles: privately printed, 1973); and Moure and Phyllis Moure, *Artists' Clubs and Exhibitions in Los Angeles before 1930.* Publications in Southern California Art, no. 2 (Los Angeles: privately printed, 1975).

bilities. The region's collectors have risen to the occasion throughout the decades, generously lending and donating American art to local institutions as well as to major national and international exhibitions. With a civic-minded spirit harking back to the first generation of local collectors in the 1920s and to the more distant generation of the 1830s, fifty-six of them are again sharing America's heritage with the public. We hope *American Paintings in Southern California Collections: From Gilbert Stuart to Georgia O'Keeffe* will encourage the continuation of this tradition, for the future of the region's museums is intimately linked with the vision of its collectors.

Ilene Susan Fort
Curator, American Art

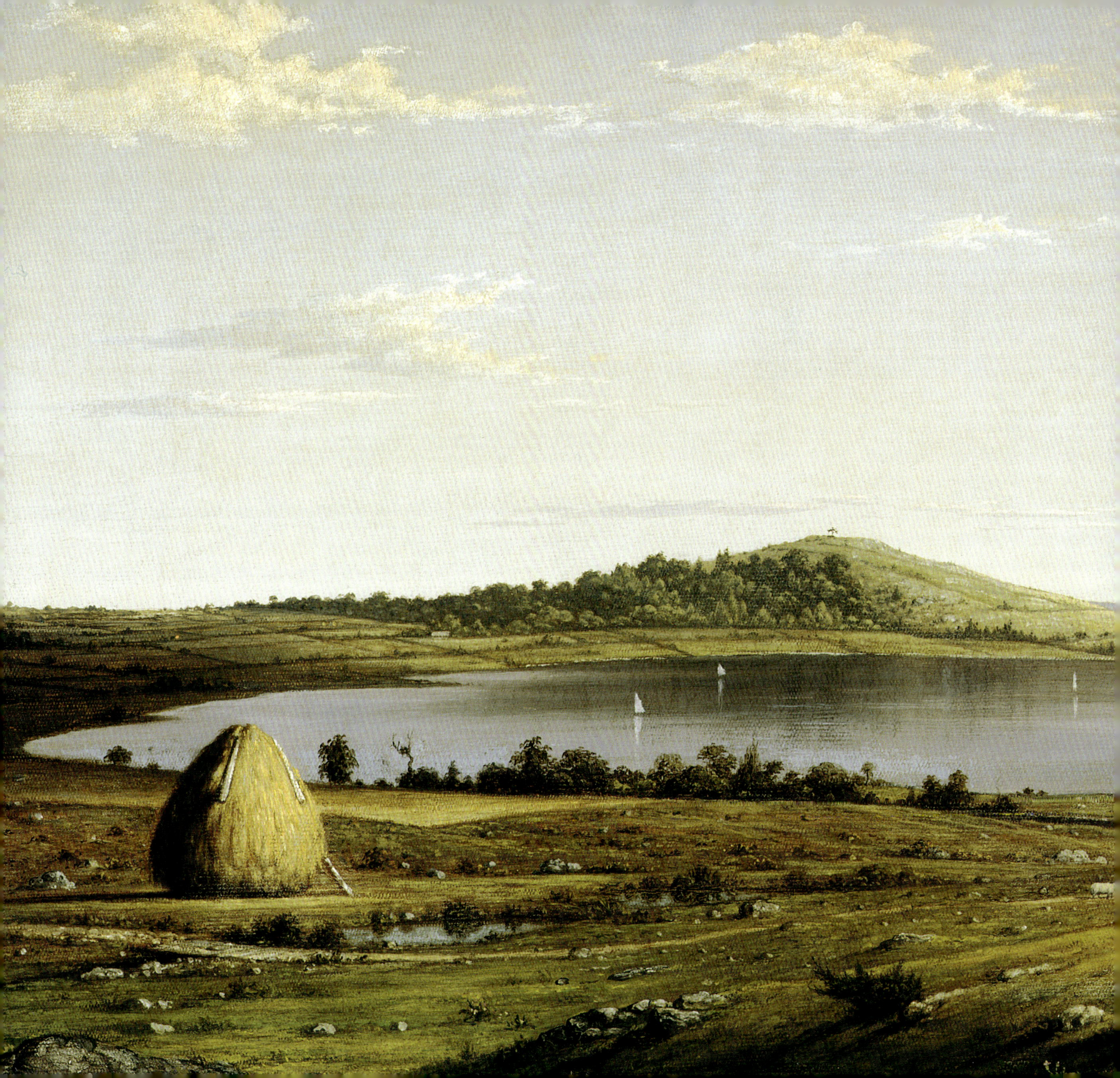

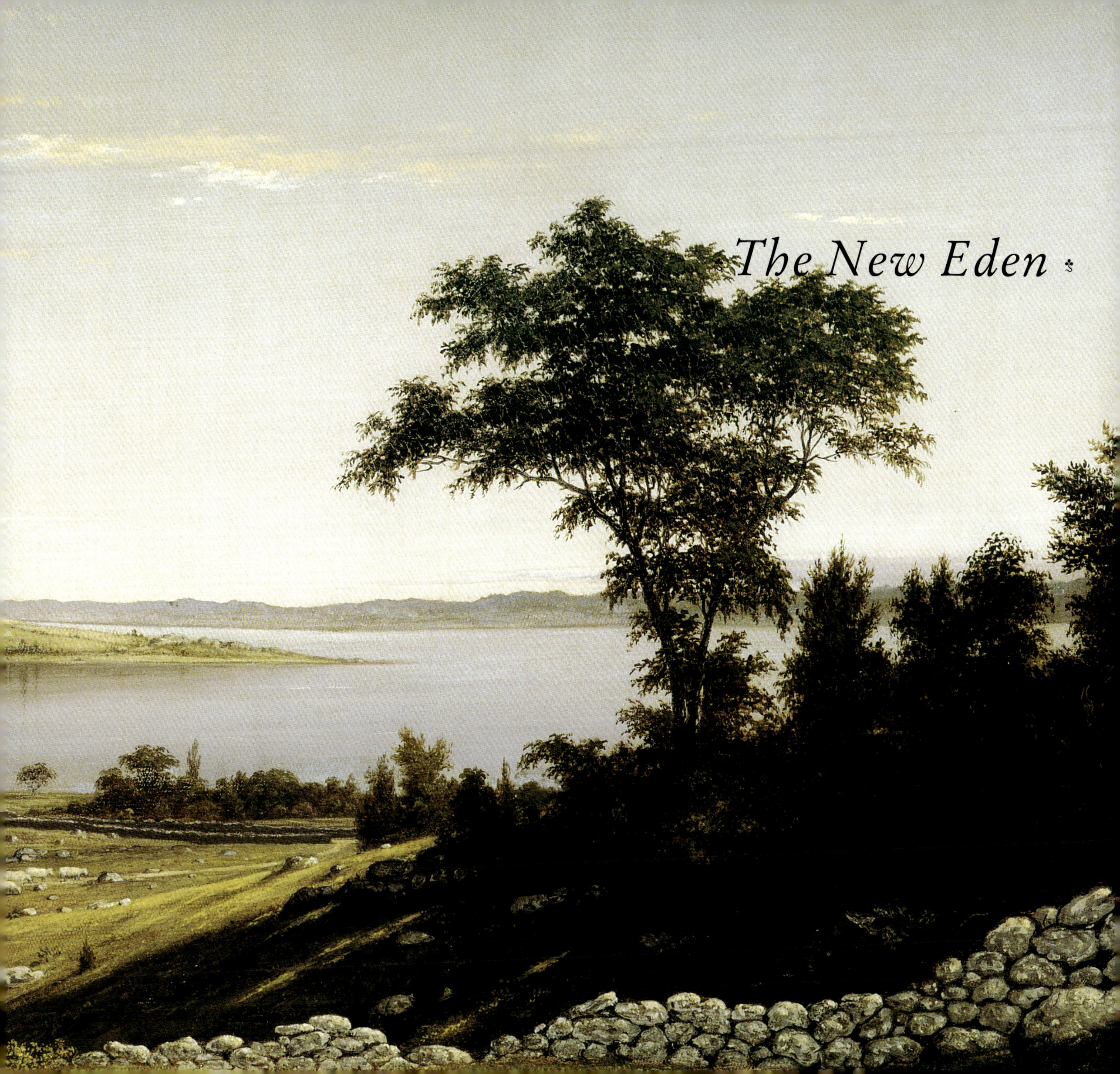

The New Eden

EUROPEAN COLONISTS establishing permanent settlements on the eastern flank of North America faced overwhelming difficulties; basic subsistence overshadowed concerns for aesthetic enhancement. Moreover, iconoclastic Puritans, who composed much of the early immigrant group, eschewed both religious iconography and superfluous decoration in their homes and churches. As portraiture provided a commemorative purpose, it was deemed one of the few acceptable forms of artistic endeavor. The early American portraitists were largely self-taught itinerant artisans who often doubled as sign and furniture painters.

(previous pages)
MARTIN JOHNSON HEADE
Rhode Island Shore
(detail)

As the colonies developed, increasing economic security allowed native-born artists to devote their time exclusively to their art. Paintings by James Peale and Gilbert Stuart portrayed many influential citizens of the newly born United States with a level of technical expertise that went beyond the naivete of the early colonial painters.

As the United States became religiously and politically more diverse, portraiture was no longer the dominant mode of artistic representation. Landscape paintings, still lifes, and representations of everyday activities began to appear. *A Dessert* (1814) by Raphaelle Peale (a nephew of James Peale) is one of the finest early American paintings of its type.

Pragmatism continued to dominate American life, and the major patronage came from prominent members of the community. History painting, the mainstay of the European academic system, traditionally depicted scenes from the Bible, classical literature, and European history. However, the absence in the United States of established religious patronage, a secure national identity, and buildings large enough to accommodate such works precluded its development here. American patrons demanded smaller paintings with less erudite themes for their homes.

The depiction of everyday life in genre scenes was a popular alternative to the more pretentious history painting. Portraying the ordinary citizen and common occurrences rather than the noble-born and events from history, genre painters celebrated the democratic aspects of the United States. Eastman Johnson and Winslow Homer captured quiet moments of rural life that appealed to Americans.

In the early part of the nineteenth century, rendering the awe-inspiring beauty of the eastern seaboard served two purposes for artists. It allowed them to expand their subject matter and at the same time to proclaim the special qualities of a land often thought of as the New Eden. Americans were determined to distinguish themselves culturally as well as politically. Images of uniquely American scenes helped to symbolize the ideals of a democratic society open to all. Thomas Doughty, an early landscapist, produced tranquil vistas, while Thomas Cole, considered the founder of the Hudson River school, depicted rugged and dramatic sites.

Spurred by the success of the Hudson River school, after midcentury many younger artists continued the American landscape tradition. Robert Duncanson, one of the best-known African American painters, combined picturesque and romantic qualities, and canvases by William Bradford, Martin Johnson Heade, and Worthington Whittredge show a growing interest in the transitory effects of nature. ❖ —T.A.

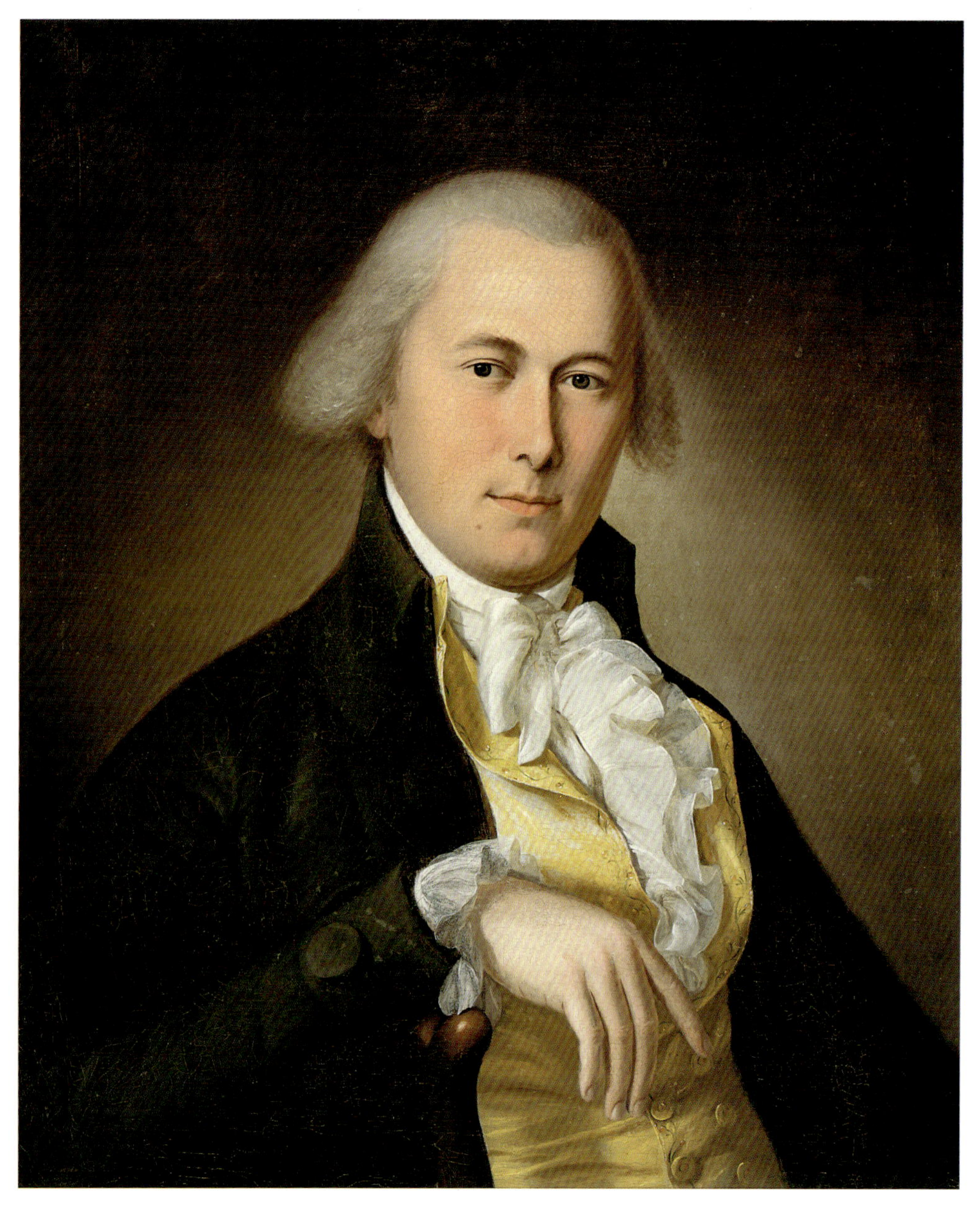

JAMES PEALE

(1749–1831)
Portrait of Samuel Allen, c. 1795–96
oil on canvas
26½ x 21½ in. (67.3 x 54.6 cm)
Mr. Craig A. Starkey

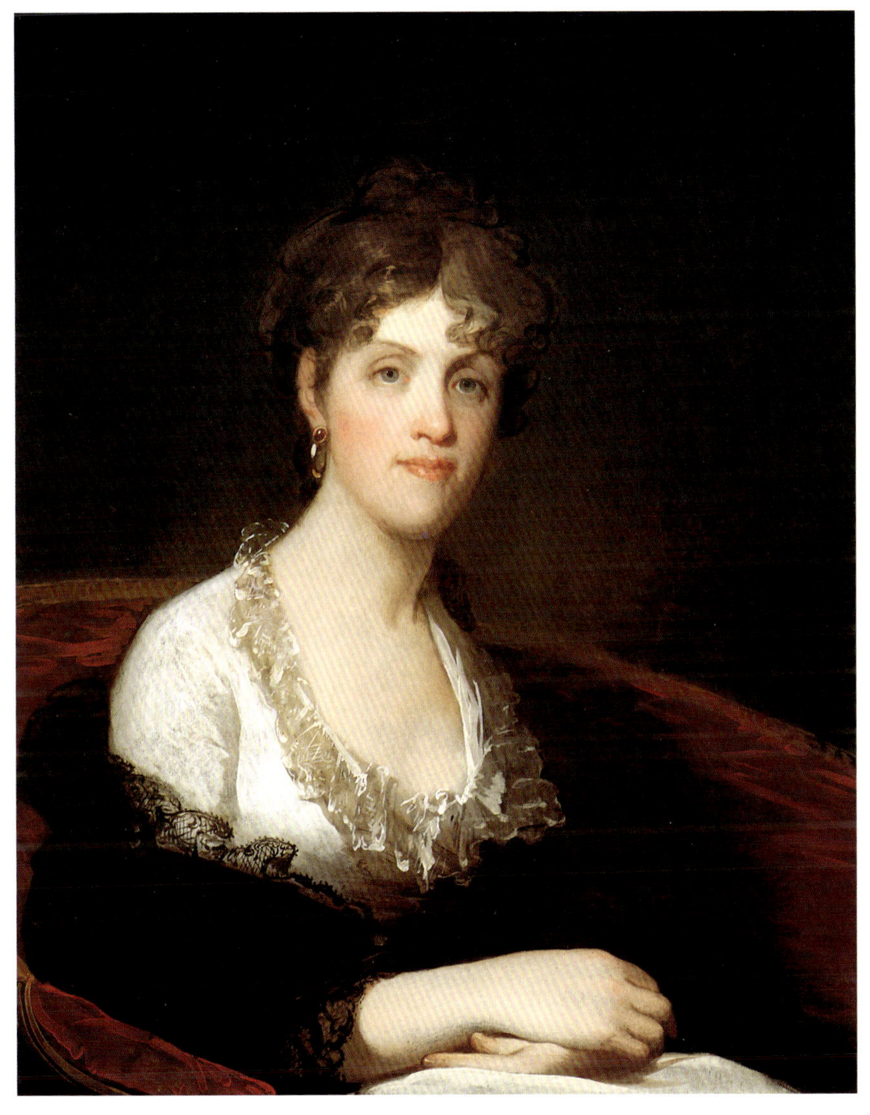

GILBERT STUART

(1755–1828)
Portrait of Mrs. Edward Penington (Helena Lawrence Holmes)
1803
oil on wood panel
28 x 22½ in. (71.1 x 57.2 cm)
Judith and Steaven Jones

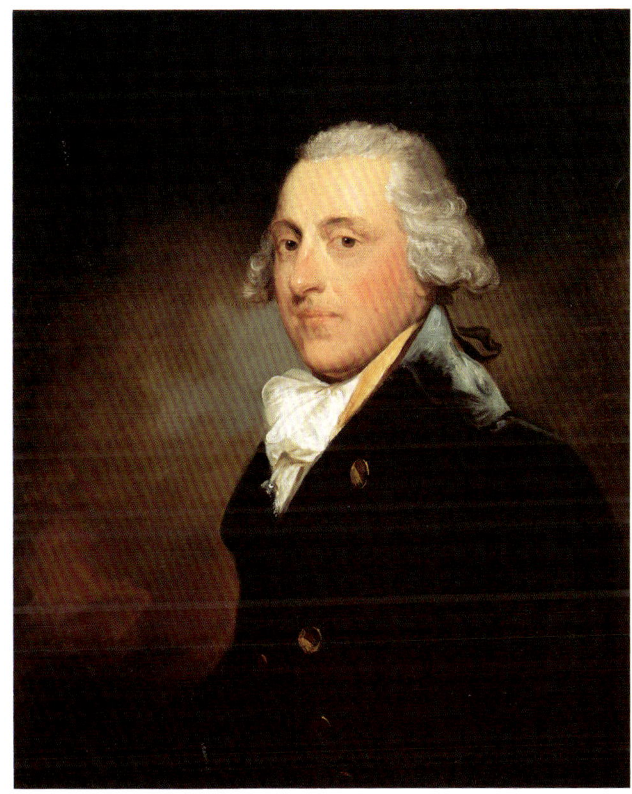

GILBERT STUART
(attributed to)

(1755–1828)
Portrait of Joshua Waddington, n.d.
oil on canvas
28½ x 24 in. (72.4 x 61 cm)
Christopher and Gretchen Ward

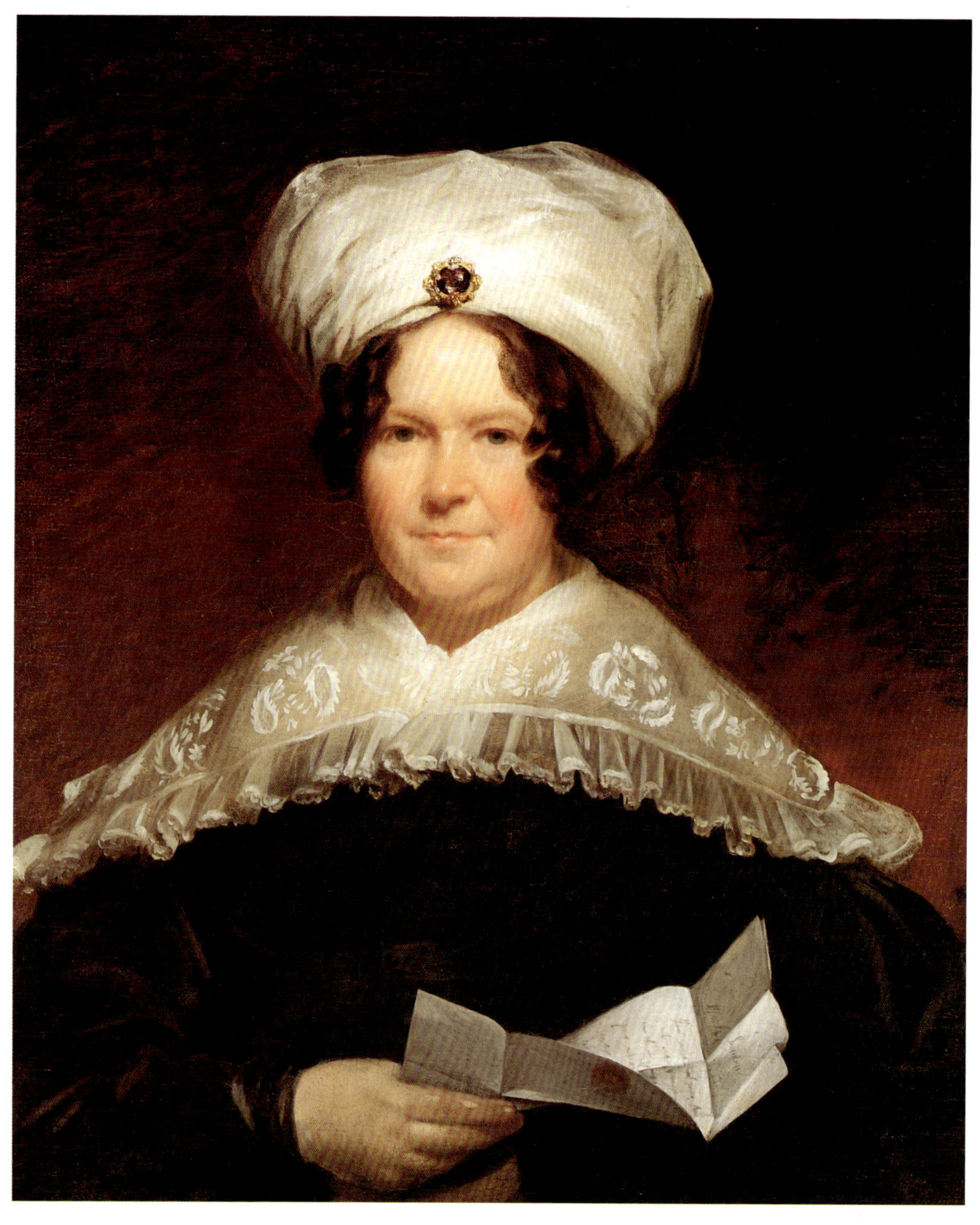

CHESTER HARDING

(1792–1866)
Portrait of Hannah Parker Willis, 1831
oil on canvas
30 x 25 in. (76.2 x 63.5 cm)
Mrs. Edward W. Carter

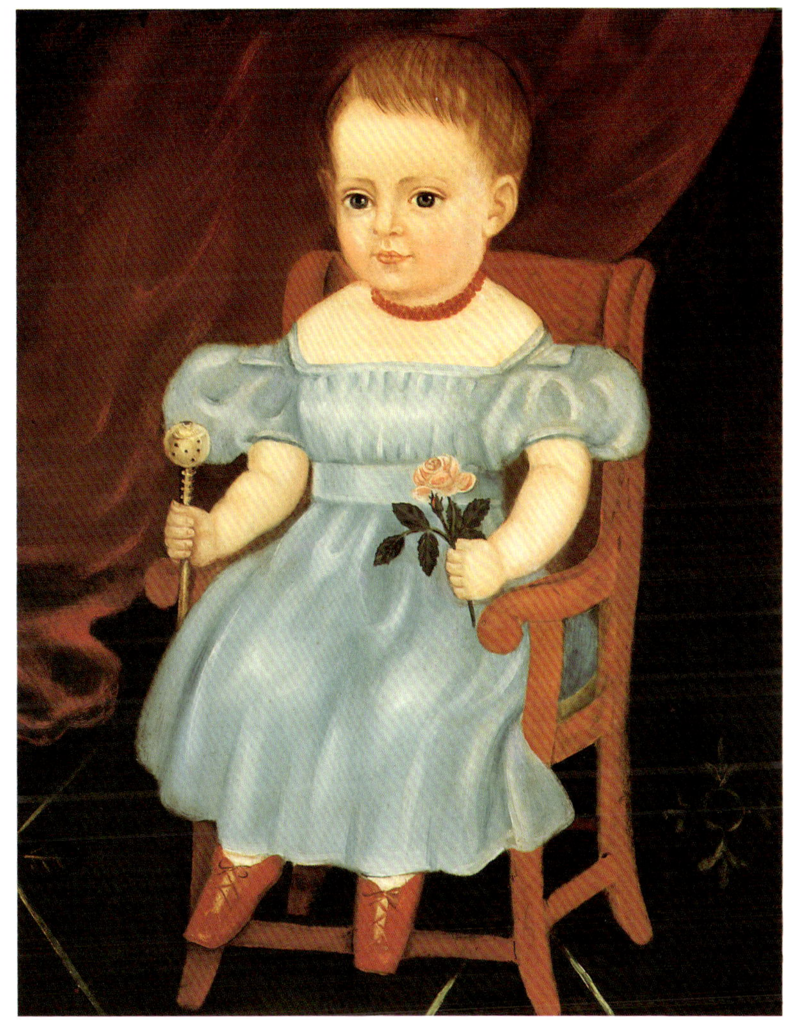

ANONYMOUS

Portrait of Sarah Ann Evans, c. 1837–38
oil on wood panel
32 x 24 in. (81.3 x 61 cm)
Mrs. Thomas J. McEwan

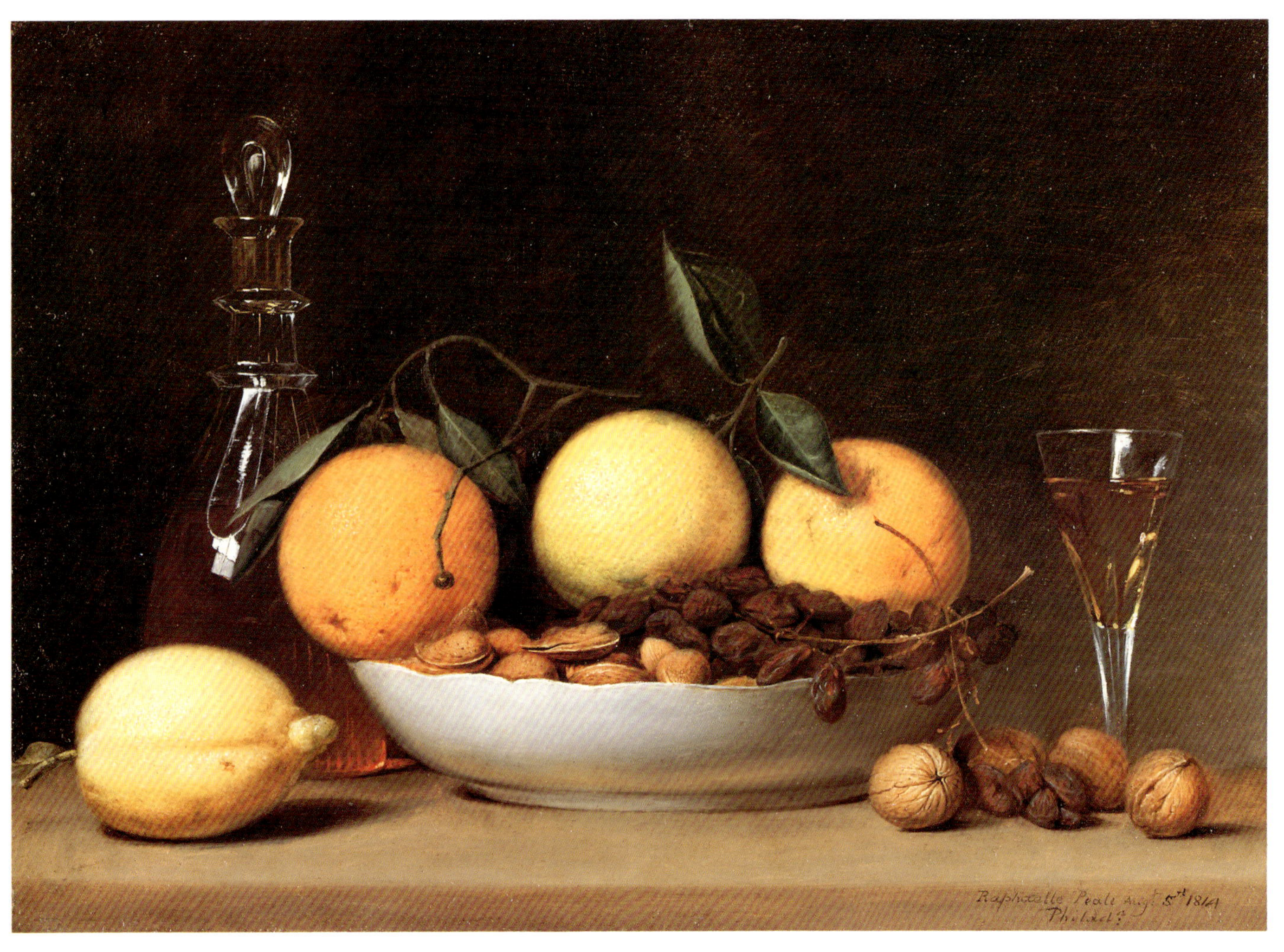

RAPHAELLE PEALE

(1774–1825)
A Dessert, 1814
oil on wood panel
13⅜ x 19 in. (34 x 48.3 cm)
Jo Ann and Julian Ganz Jr.

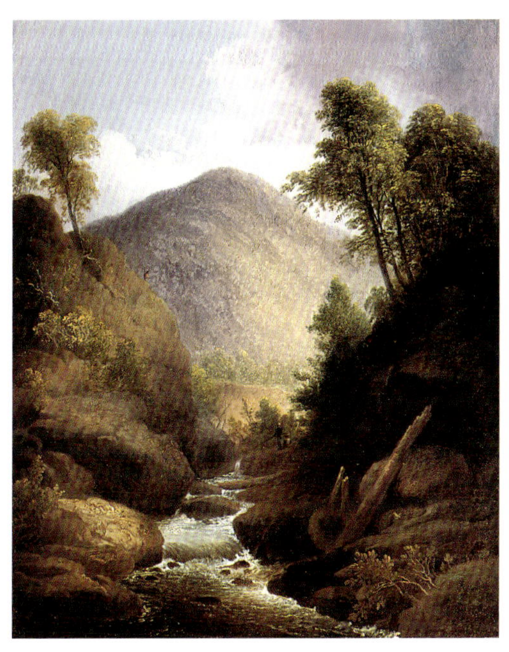

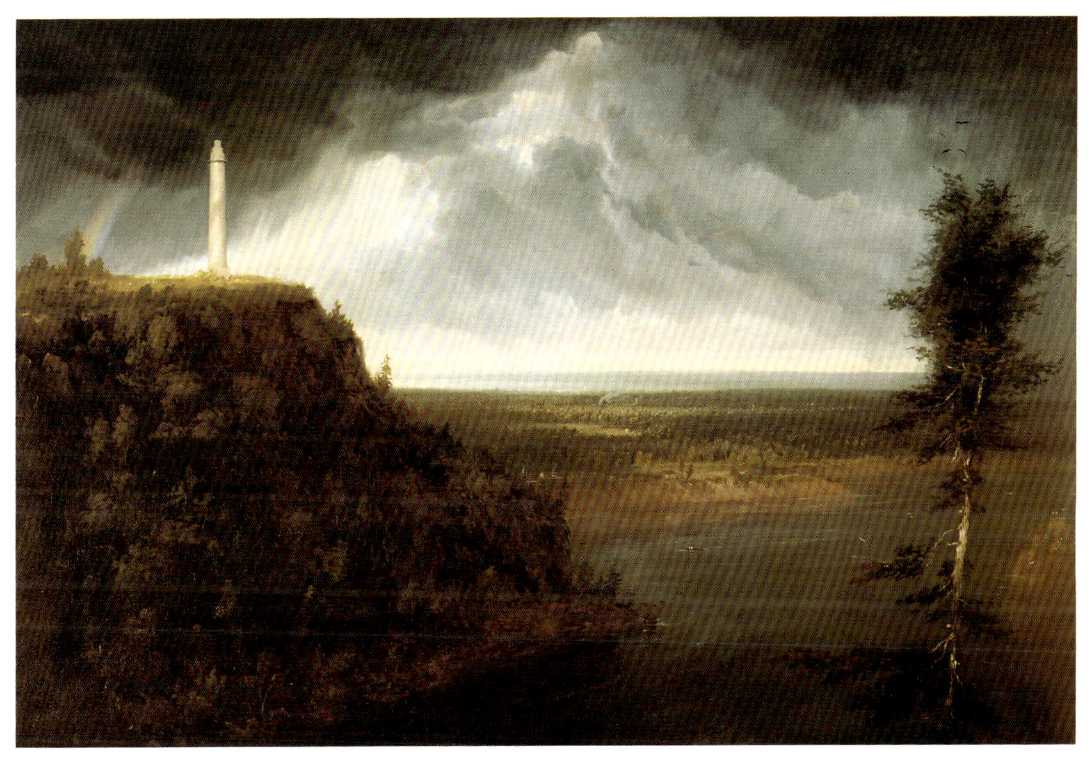

THOMAS DOUGHTY

(1793–1856)
Waterfall with Fishermen
(Fishing in the Mountains)
1836
oil on panel
18⅛ x 14½ in. (46 x 36.8 cm)
Mr. and Mrs. William M. Carpenter

THOMAS COLE

(1801–1848)
Brock's Monument, c. 1836
oil on canvas
29¾ x 44½ in. (75.7 x 113 cm)
Dr. Herbert and Elizabeth Sussman

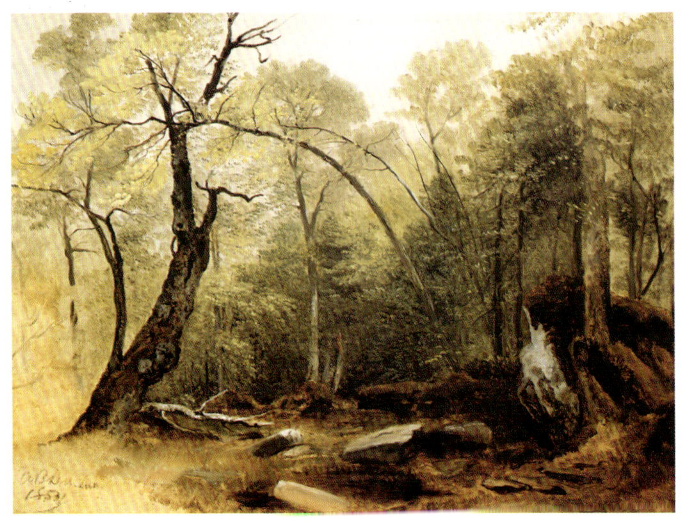

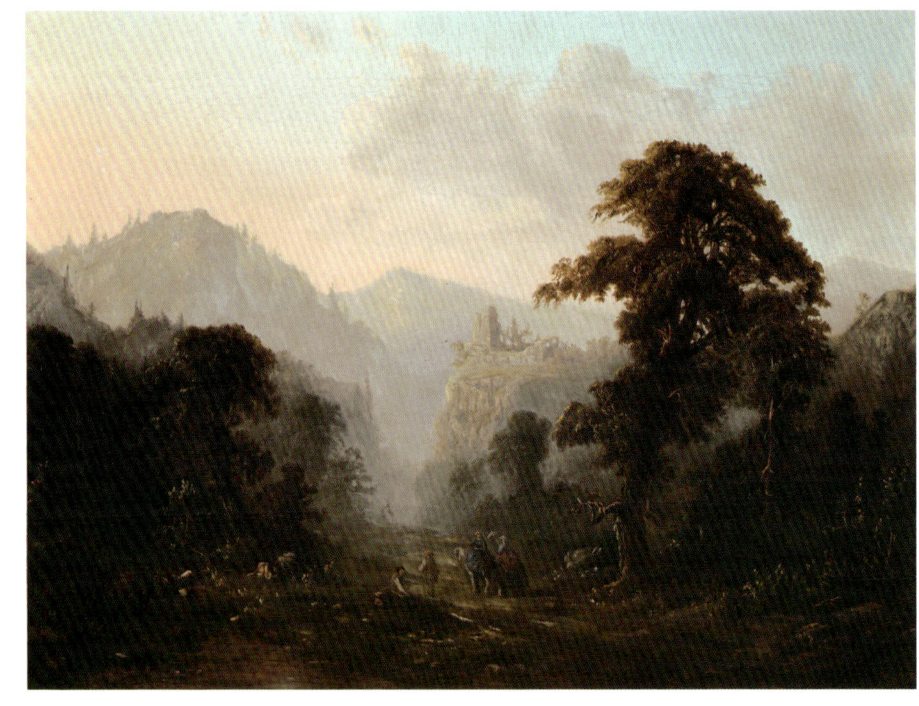

ASHER B. DURAND

(1796–1886)
Study in the Woods, 1853
oil on canvas
18 x 24 in. (45.7 x 61 cm)
Nancy and Arthur Manella

ROBERT DUNCANSON

(1821–1872)
Landscape with Ruin, c. 1853
oil on canvas
24 x 32 in. (61 x 81.3 cm)
Bram and Sandra Dijkstra

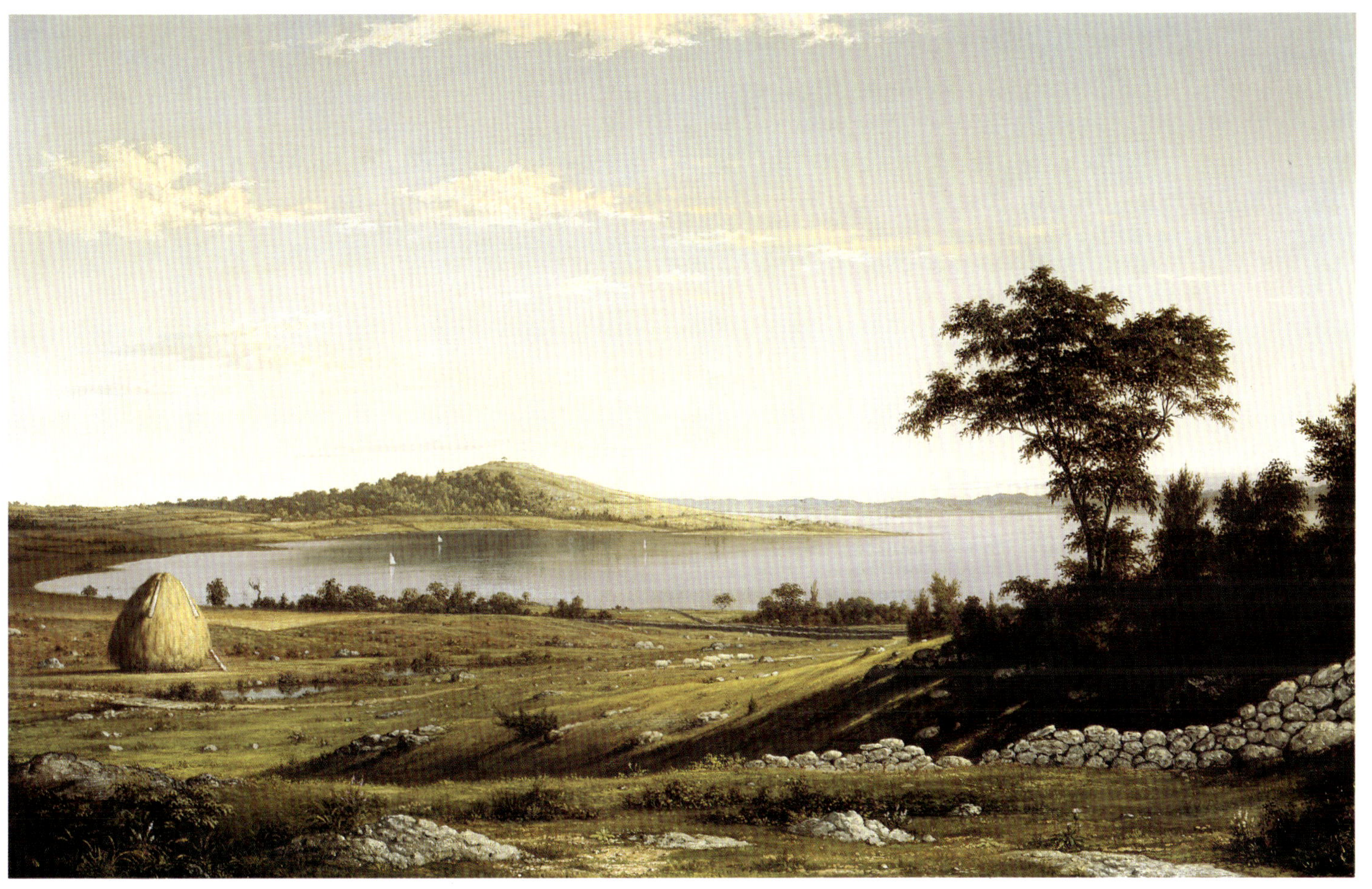

MARTIN JOHNSON HEADE

(1819–1904)
Rhode Island Shore, 1858
oil on canvas
20¼ x 32¼ in. (51.4 x 81.9 cm)
Los Angeles County Museum of Art,
gift of Charles C. and Elma Ralphs Shoemaker

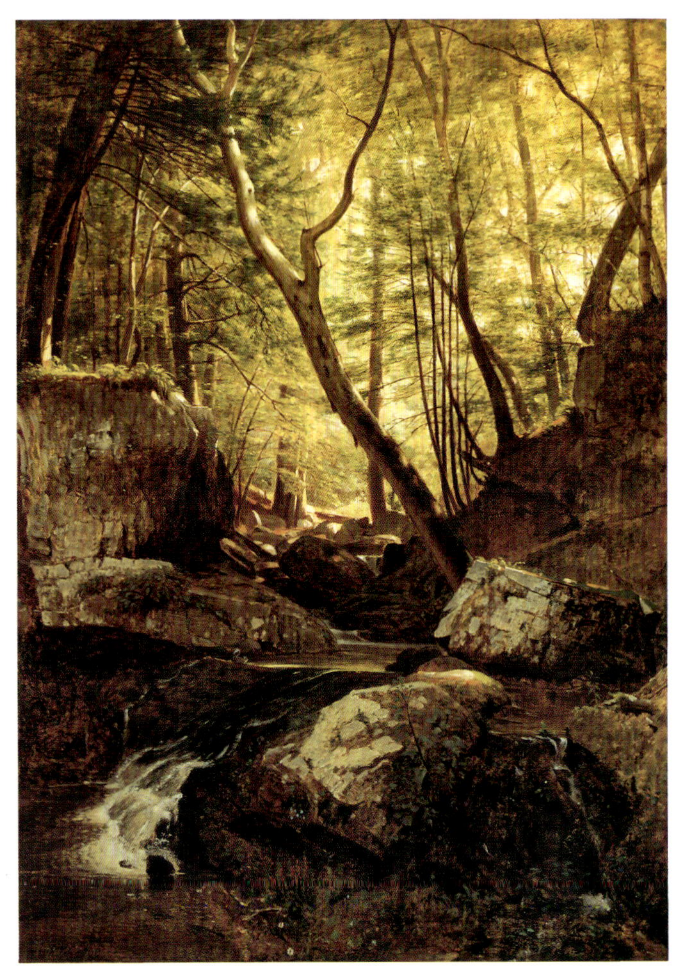

WORTHINGTON WHITTREDGE

(1820–1910)
Kaatskill Creek, c. 1882
oil on canvas
27 x 19½ in. (68.6 x 49.5 cm)
Dr. and Mrs. M. S. Mickiewicz

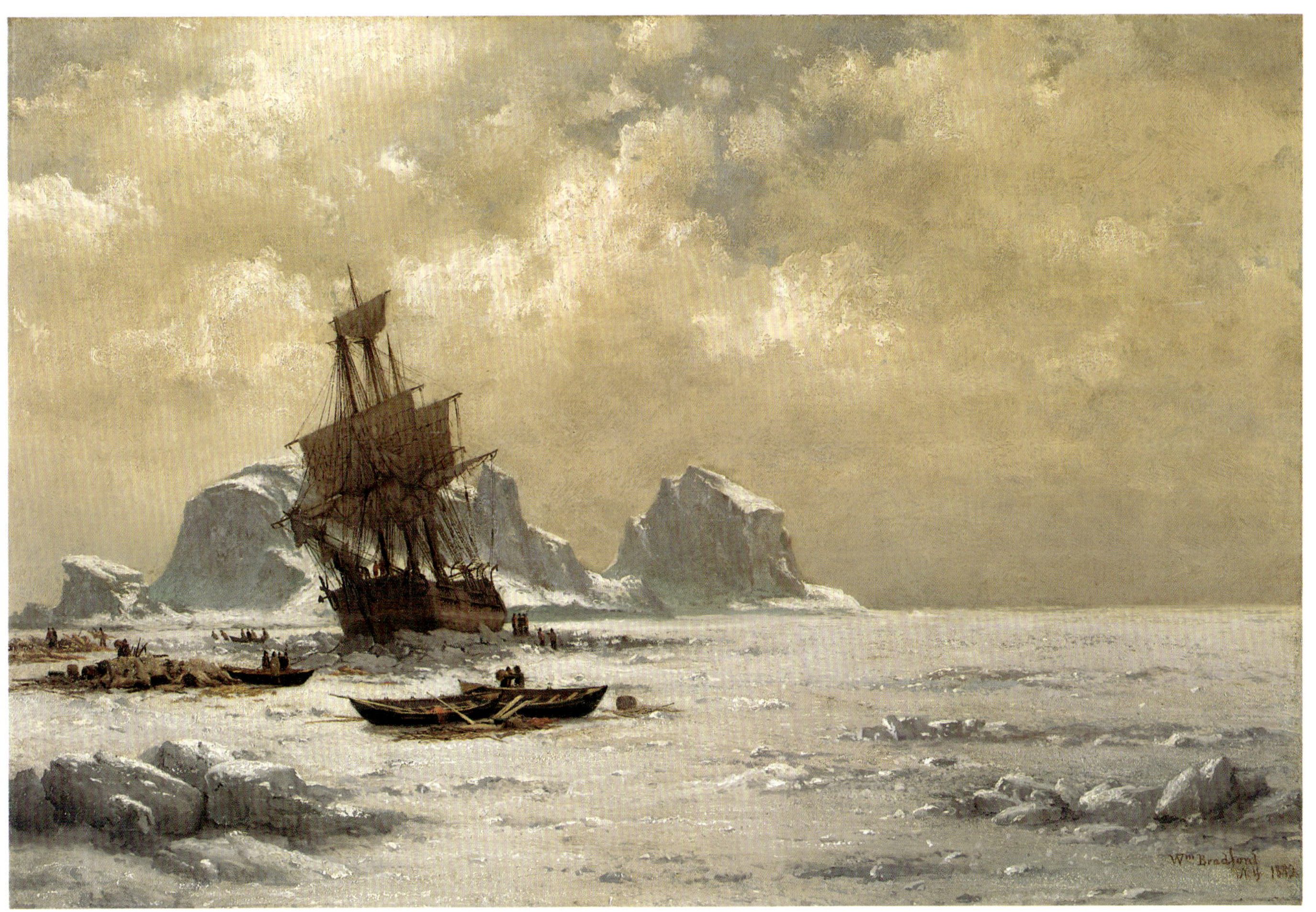

WILLIAM BRADFORD

(1823–1892)
Caught in the Ice, 1882
oil on canvas
19½ x 29½ in. (49.5 x 75 cm)
Theodore G. and Eleanor S. Congdon

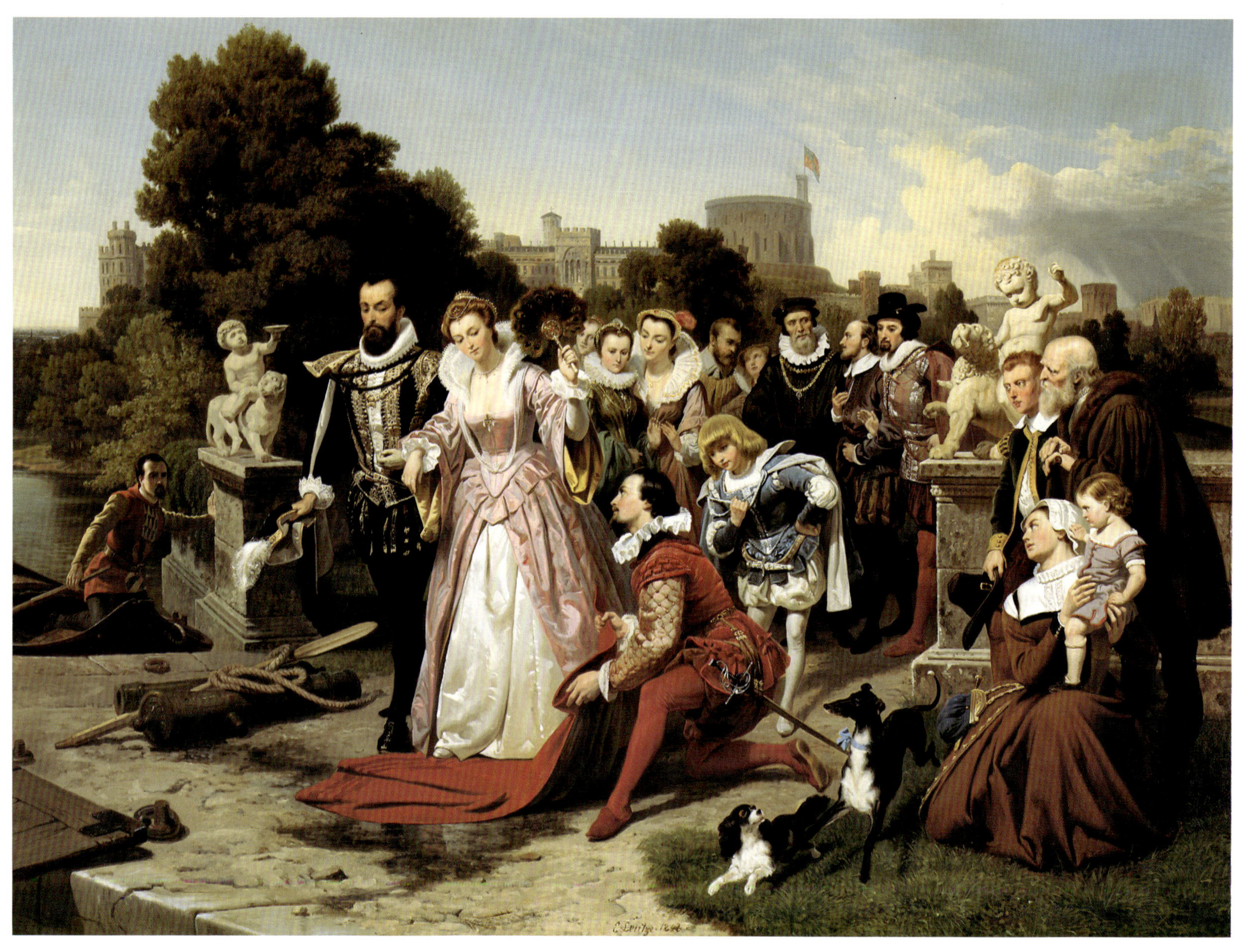

EMANUEL LEUTZE

(1816–1868)
Elizabeth and Raleigh, 1848
oil on canvas
48 x 66 in. (121.9 x 167.6 cm)
private collection

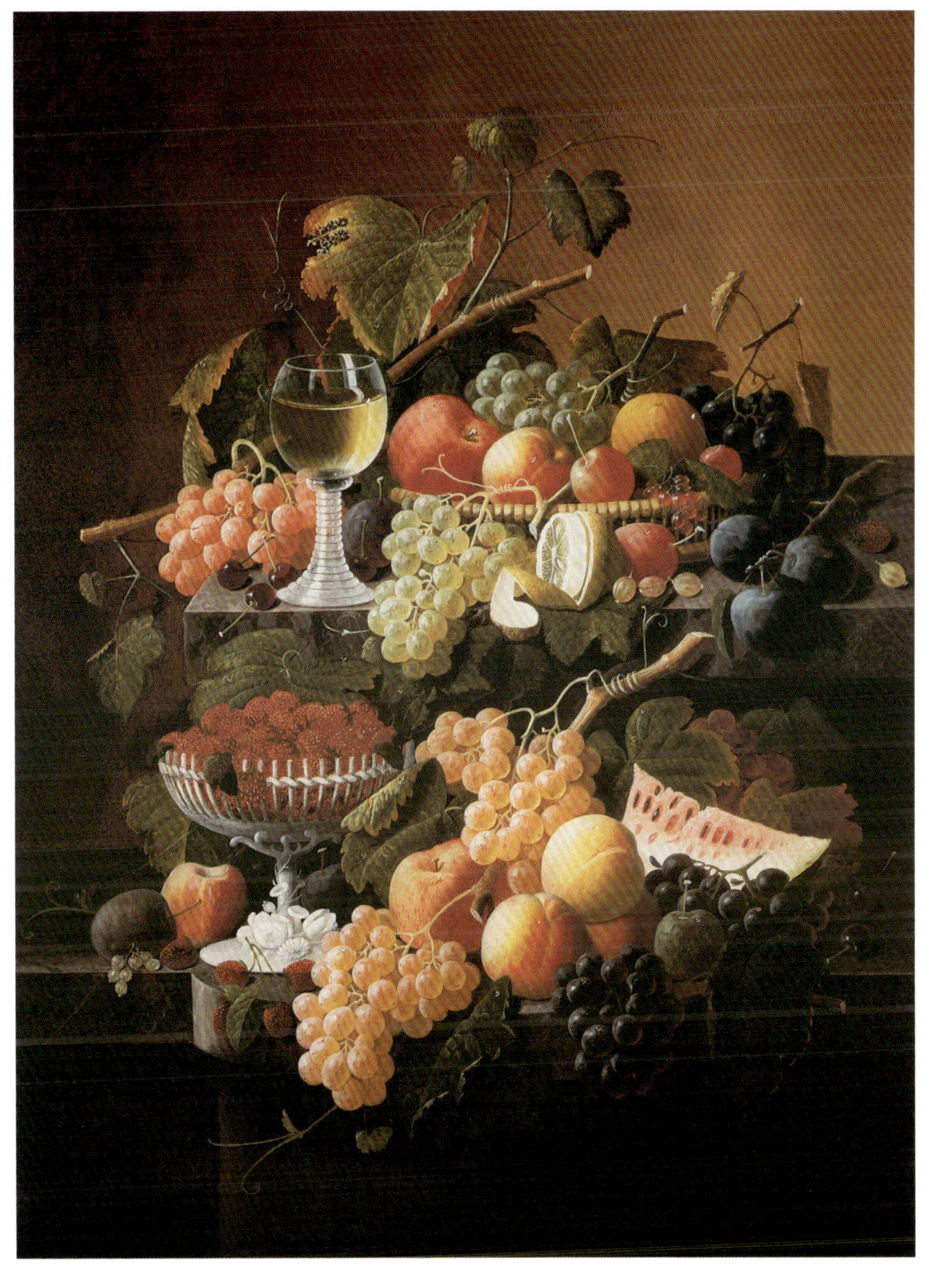

SEVERIN ROESEN

(1815/16–1872)
Still Life, n.d.
oil on canvas
39½ x 29 in. (100.3 x 73.7 cm)
Mrs. Cecile C. Bartman

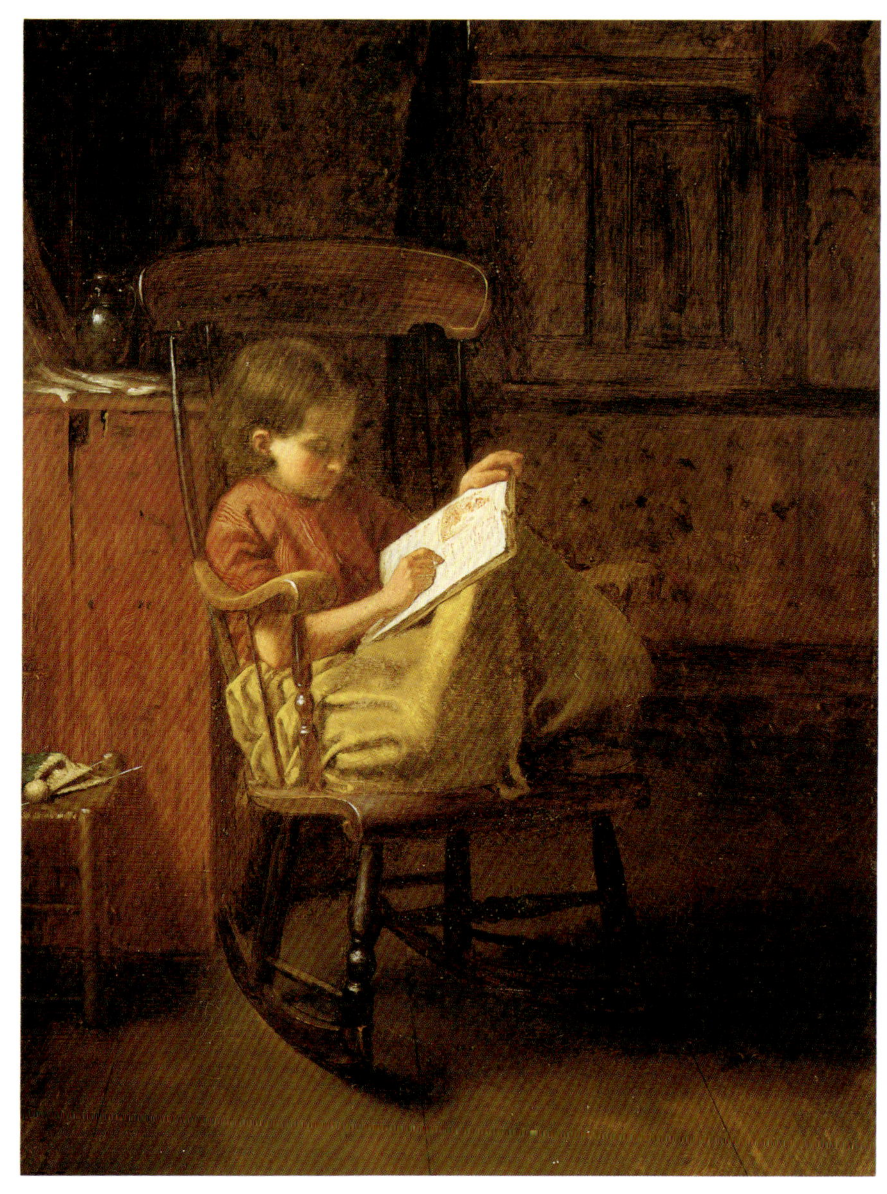

EASTMAN JOHNSON

(1824–1906)
The Boston Rocker, late 1860s – early 1870s
oil on board
19½ x 14¾ in. (49.5 x 37.5 cm)
Bernard Solomon

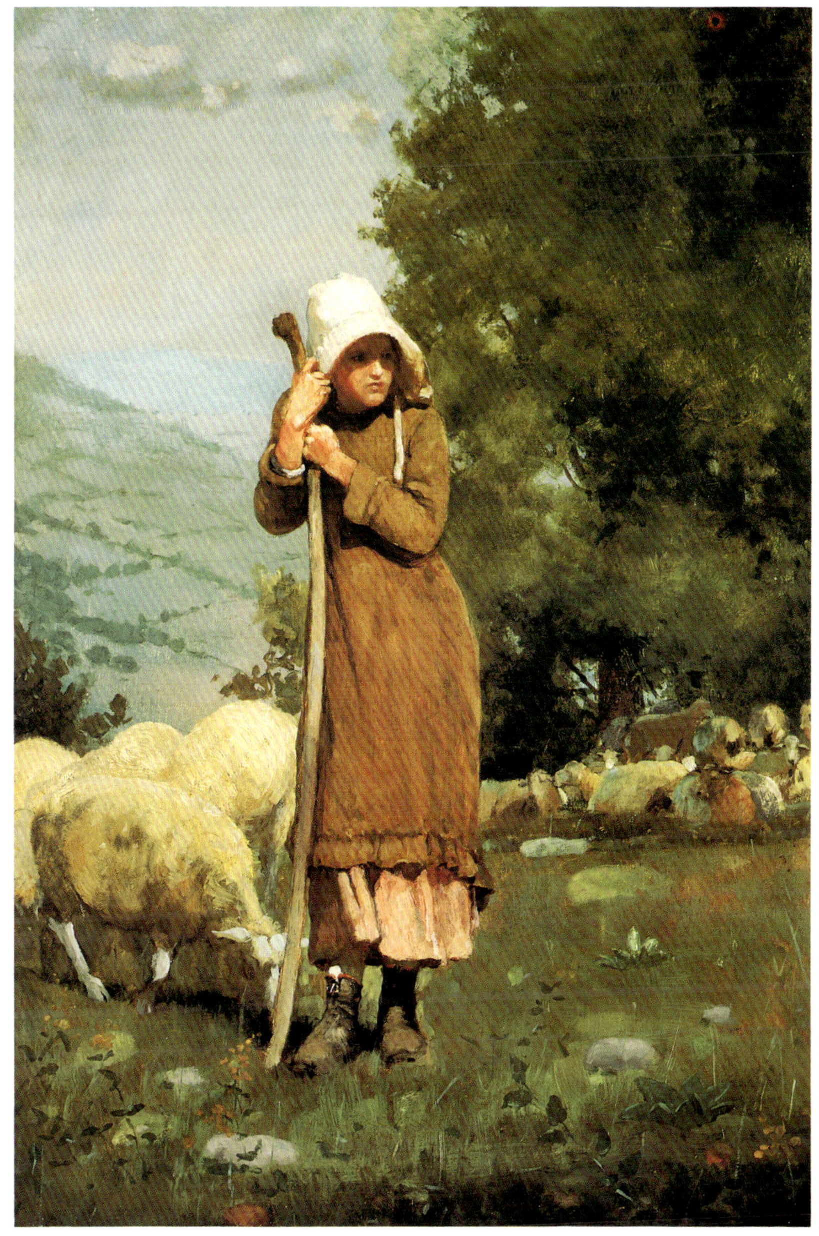

WINSLOW HOMER

(1836–1910)
The Shepherdess, 1879
oil on canvas
22¾ x 15½ in. (57.8 x 39.4 cm)
Mr. and Mrs. J. Douglas Pardee

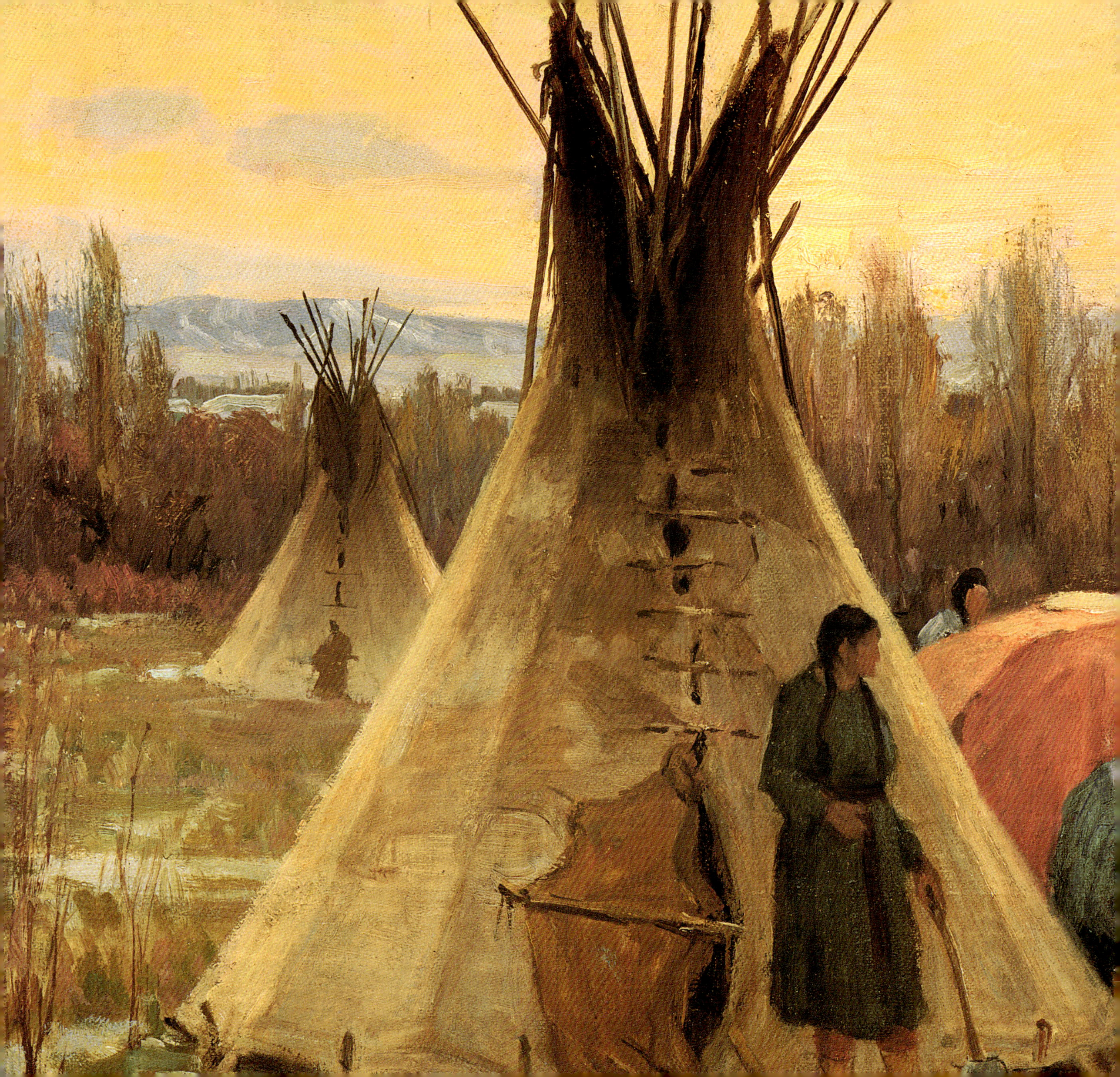

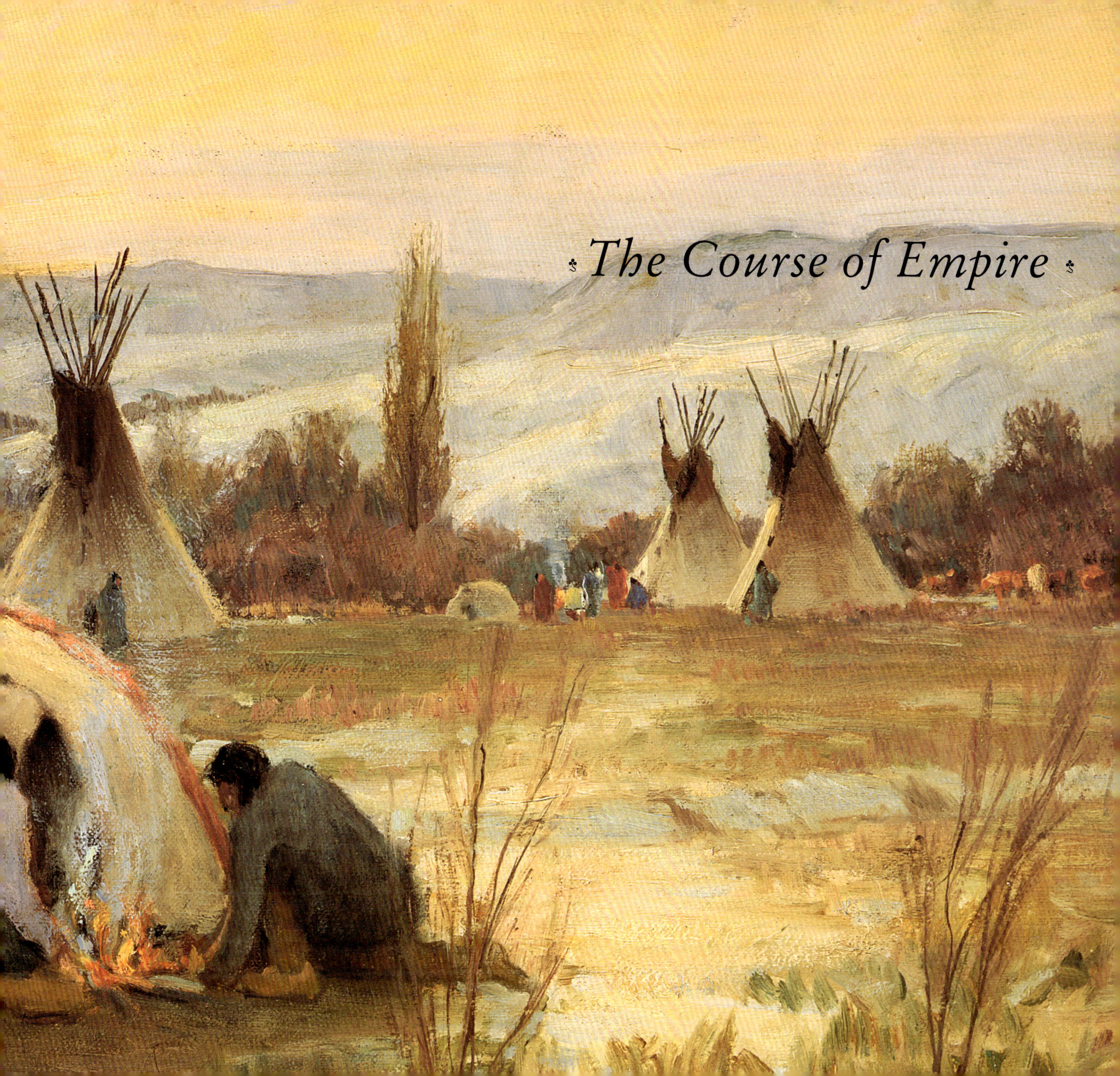

The Course of Empire

AS THE COUNTRY matured and expanded geographically, the wide open West was appealing to the waves of European immigrants and to native-born citizens who wanted to make a new start. The sense of Manifest Destiny, a belief that divine will coincided with the expansion of American civilization from coast to coast, added momentum to nationalistic ideals. As eastern landscape sites became familiar to American art patrons and viewers, artists too traveled west to find new vistas.

In the early part of the nineteenth century, expeditions to the West were generally under military command; they were often involved in boundary disputes as well as establishing overland routes for railroads and settlers. Artists often accompanied these expeditions and depicted the varied terrain and inhabitants. When gold was discovered in California in 1848, hopes of instant wealth fueled a generation of migrants to the West.

(previous pages)
JOSEPH HENRY SHARP
Crow Encampment (Spring Morning near Custer Mountain)
(detail)

After the Civil War, settlement, tourism, and commercial expansion sent ever greater multitudes to the new states and territories. The visual novelty of these landscapes—vast deserts, rolling prairies, vaulting mountain ranges—lured many highly trained artists west to portray what was still conceived of by Easterners as a mysterious, wild, and exotic land of unfamiliar peoples and customs. Large-scale paintings of such sites as Yosemite and Yellowstone were often presented in special exhibitions for eastern audiences, complete with theatrical sets and brochures explaining the scene. In 1871 Thomas Moran accompanied a geological survey team commissioned by the government to map the Yellowstone territory. His watercolors of the area encouraged its preservation as the first national park, helping to make it an indelible part of American consciousness. In paintings like *The Green River, Wyoming* (1879) Moran brought the West's grandeur within the reach of the eastern viewer.

By the 1880s the frontier way of life was beginning to disappear. Mexico had lost control of California. The Centennial had encouraged a romanticized view of the country's past. The dashing vaqueros, so common in earlier times, suggest a picturesque nostalgia in William Hahn's *Mexican Cattle Drive in Southern California* (1883). But it was Frederic Remington, more than any other artist, who around the turn of the century shaped our memory of the Wild West. An Easterner, Remington produced dramatically heightened depictions of Native Americans and especially the mythic life of the Western cowboy and soldier.

In the late nineteenth century, federal policies for Indian assimilation led to the decline in Native American culture. Though earlier American artists had traveled west to document the indigenous peoples and their traditions, in the early twentieth century painters such as E. Irving Couse, Maynard Dixon, and Joseph Henry Sharp, working in the Southwest, sought to record the customs of these proud peoples before their traditional ways of life disappeared forever. ❖ —T.A.

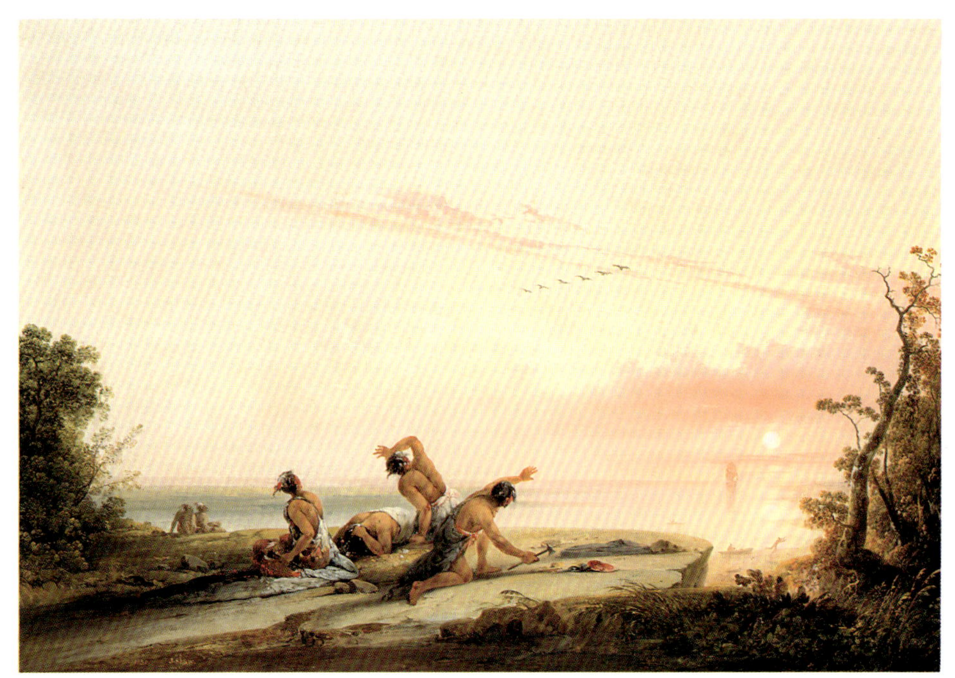

JOSHUA SHAW

(1776–1860)
The Coming of the White Man, 1850
oil on canvas
25¼ x 36⅜ in. (64.1 x 92.4 cm)
Elisabeth Waldo-Dentzel,
courtesy of the Multicultural Music/Art Foundation
of Northridge

THOMAS MORAN

(1837–1926)
The Green River, Wyoming, 1879
oil on canvas
26 x 62 in. (66 x 157.5 cm)
private collection

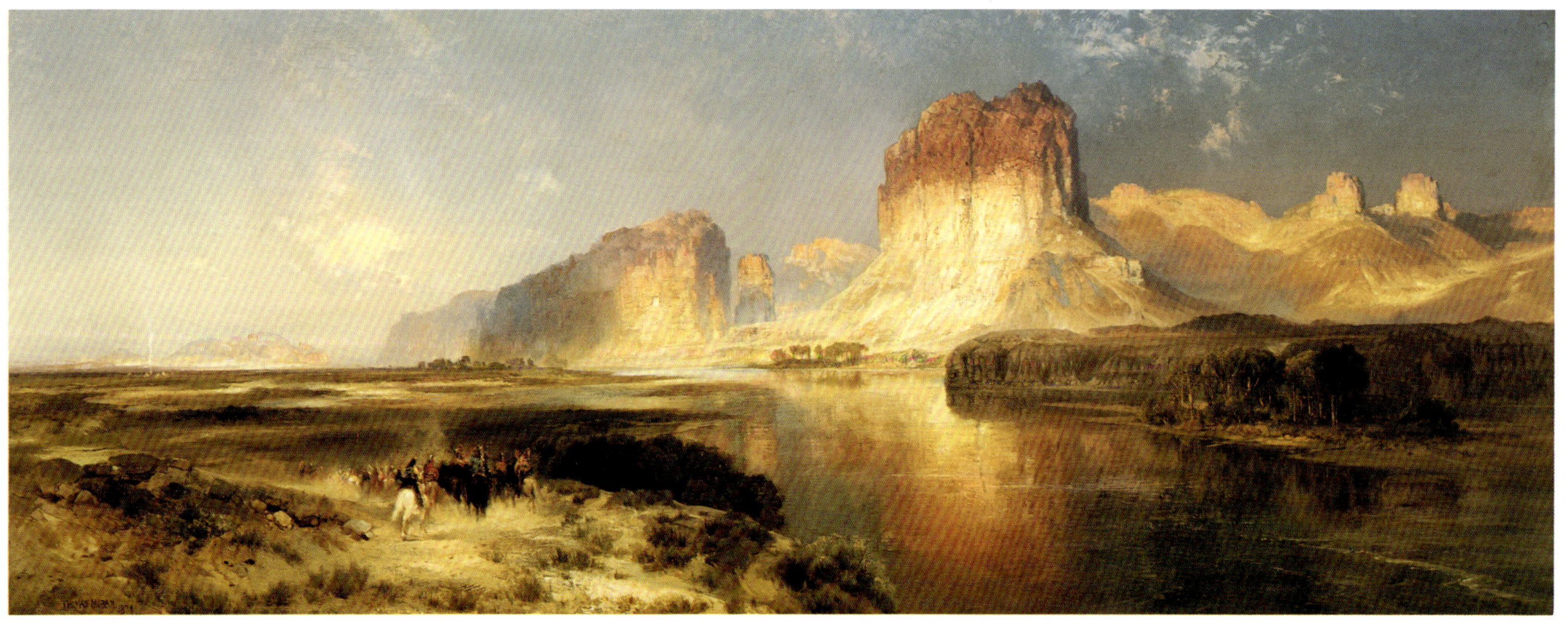

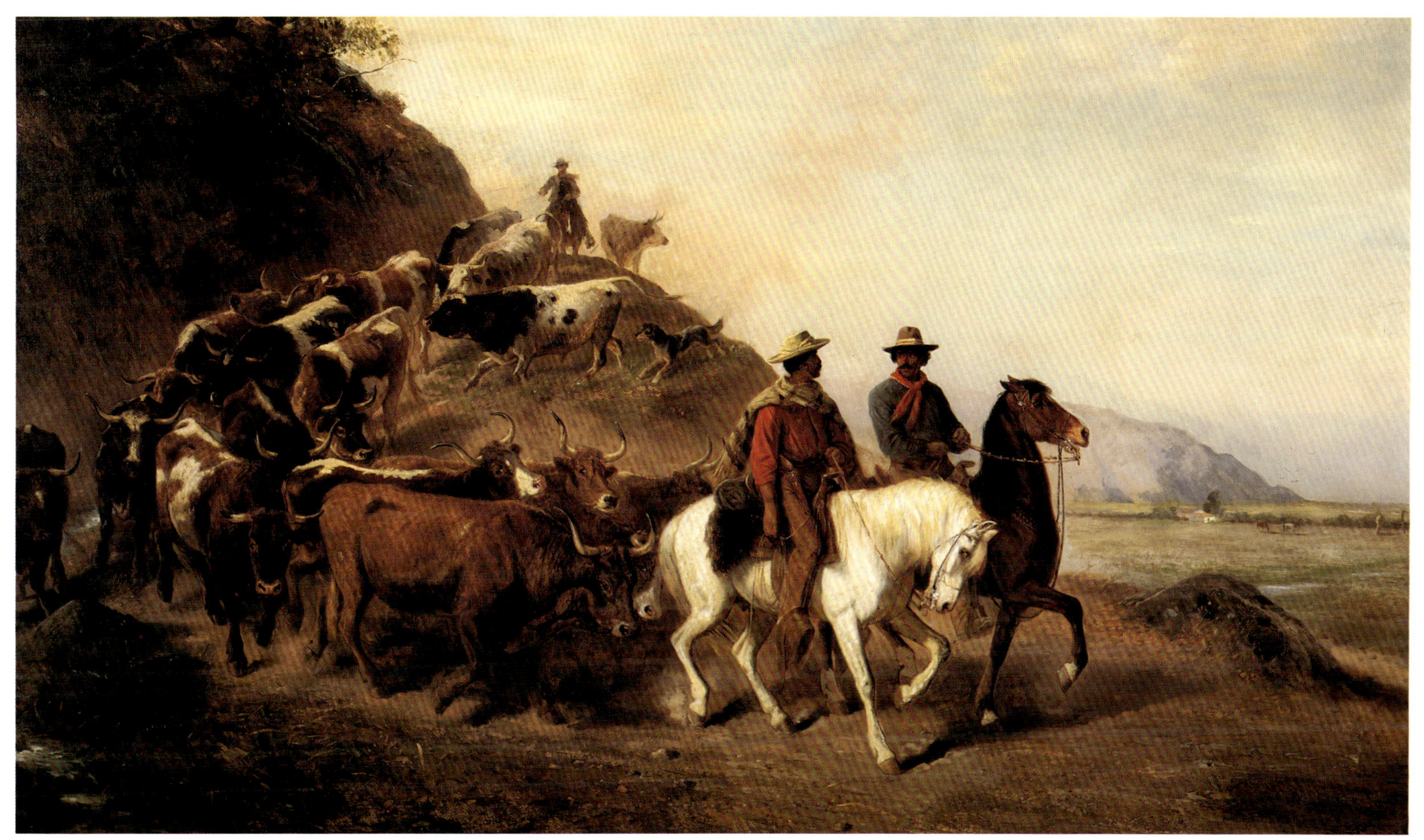

WILLIAM HAHN

(1829–1887)

Mexican Cattle Drive in Southern California, 1883

oil on canvas

34½ x 60 in. (86.4 x 152.4 cm)

Dr. and Mrs. Edward H. Boseker

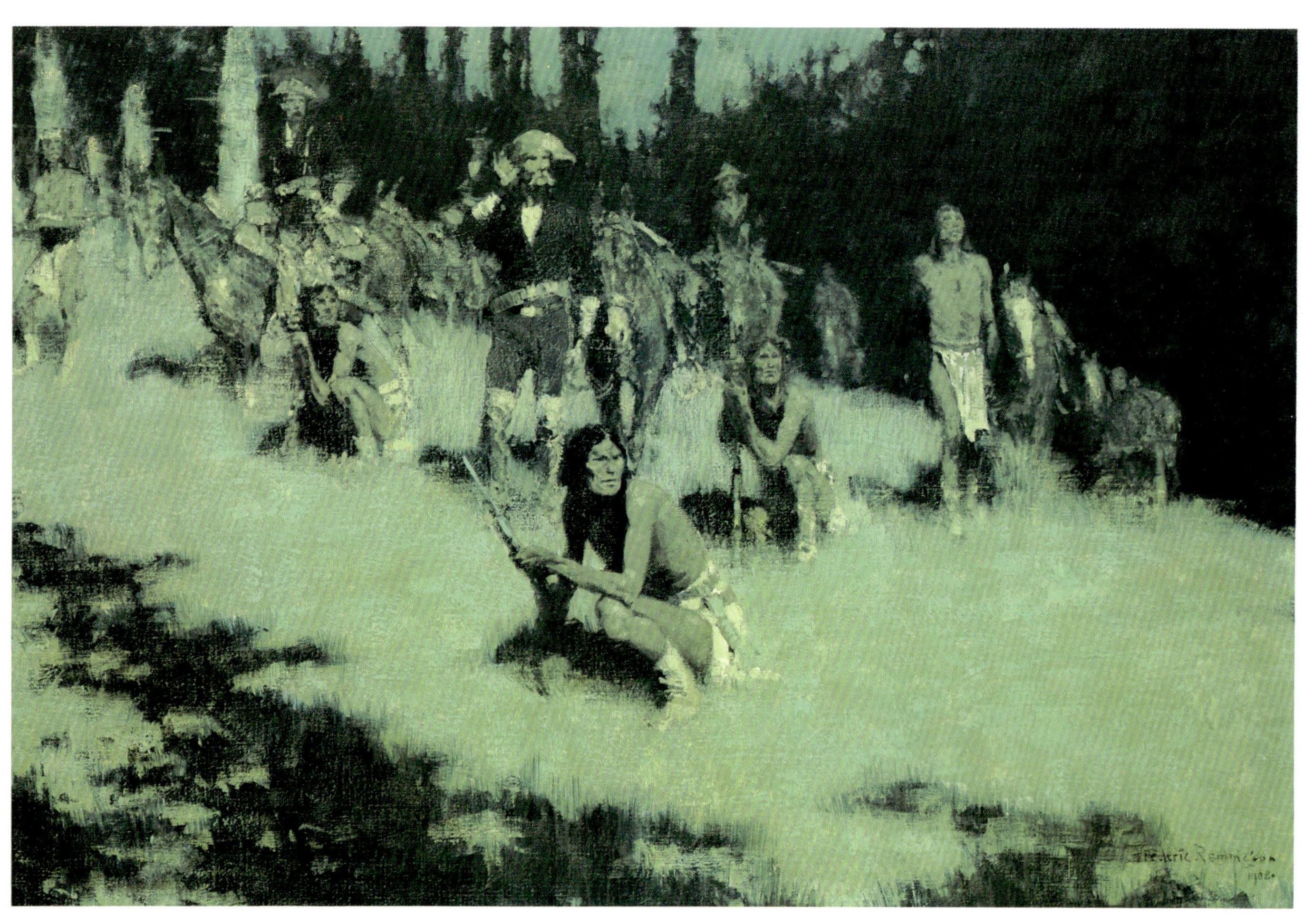

FREDERIC REMINGTON

(1861–1909)
Apache Scouts Listening, 1908
oil on canvas
27 x 40 in. (68.6 x 101.6 cm)
private collection

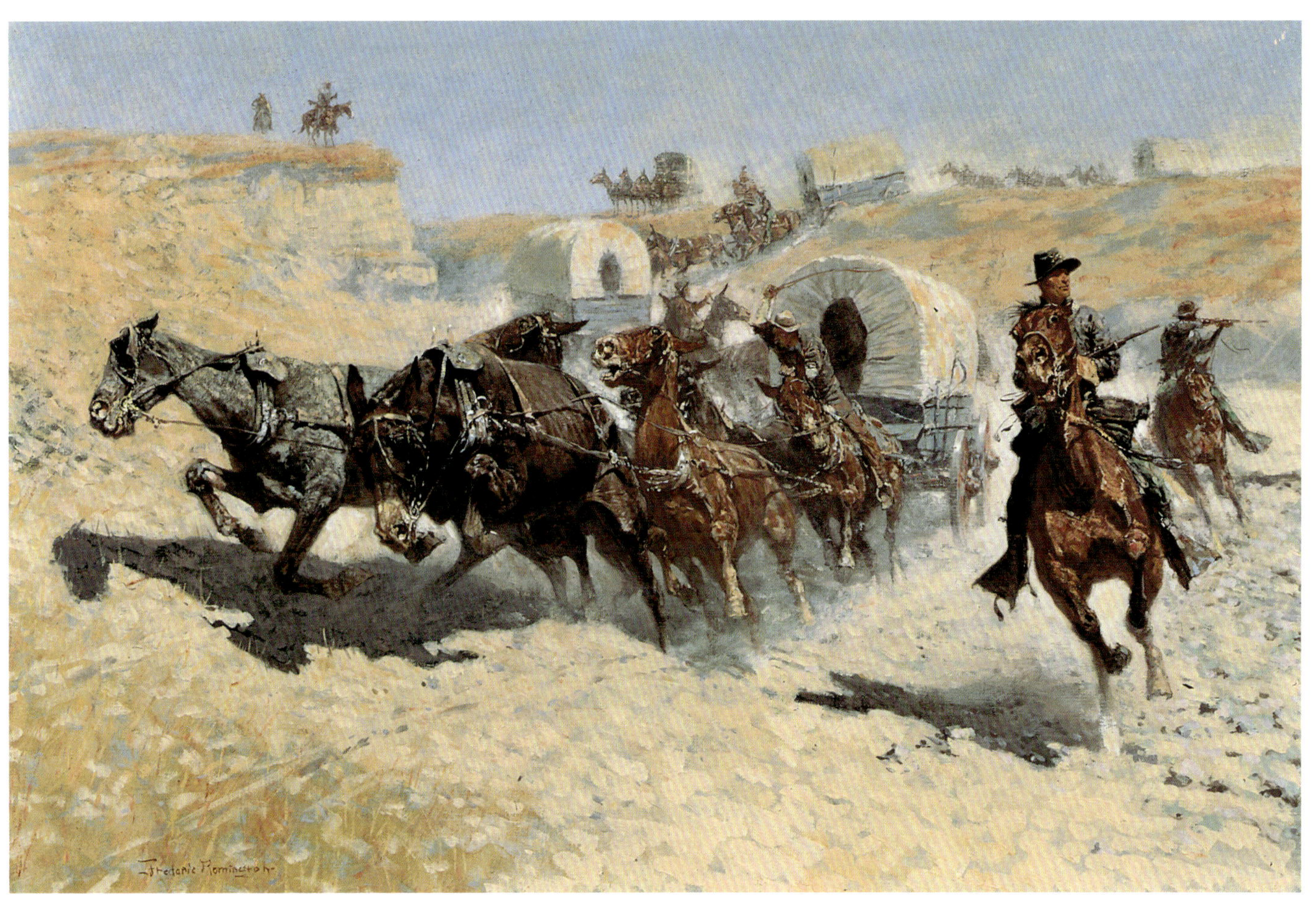

FREDERIC REMINGTON

(1861–1909)
Attack on the Supply Wagons, c. 1905
oil on canvas
30 x 45½ in. (76.2 x 115.6 cm)
private collection,
courtesy Guggenheim, Asher Associates Inc.

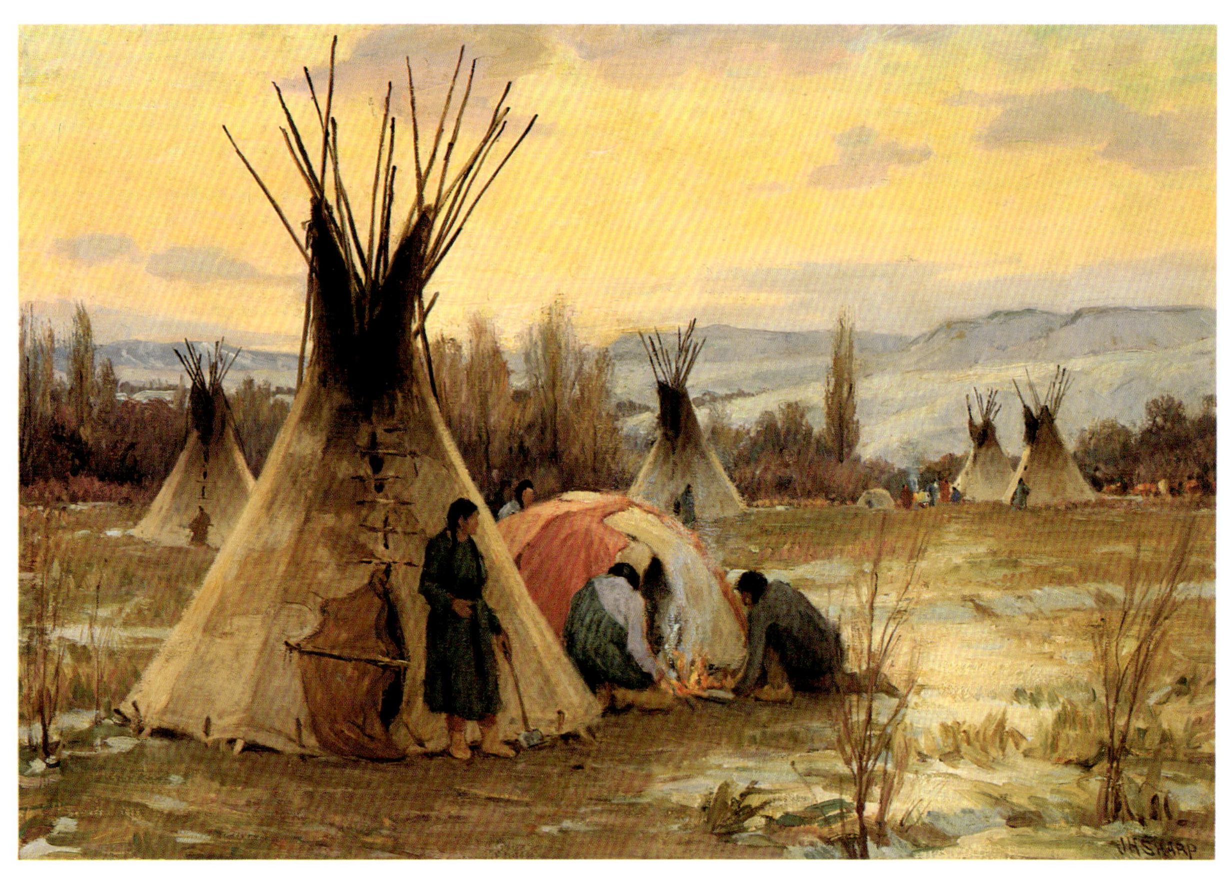

JOSEPH HENRY SHARP

(1859–1953)
Crow Encampment (Spring Morning near Custer Mountain), n.d.
oil on canvas
18½ x 26 in. (47 x 66 cm)
Samuel and Elaine Rosenthal Trust

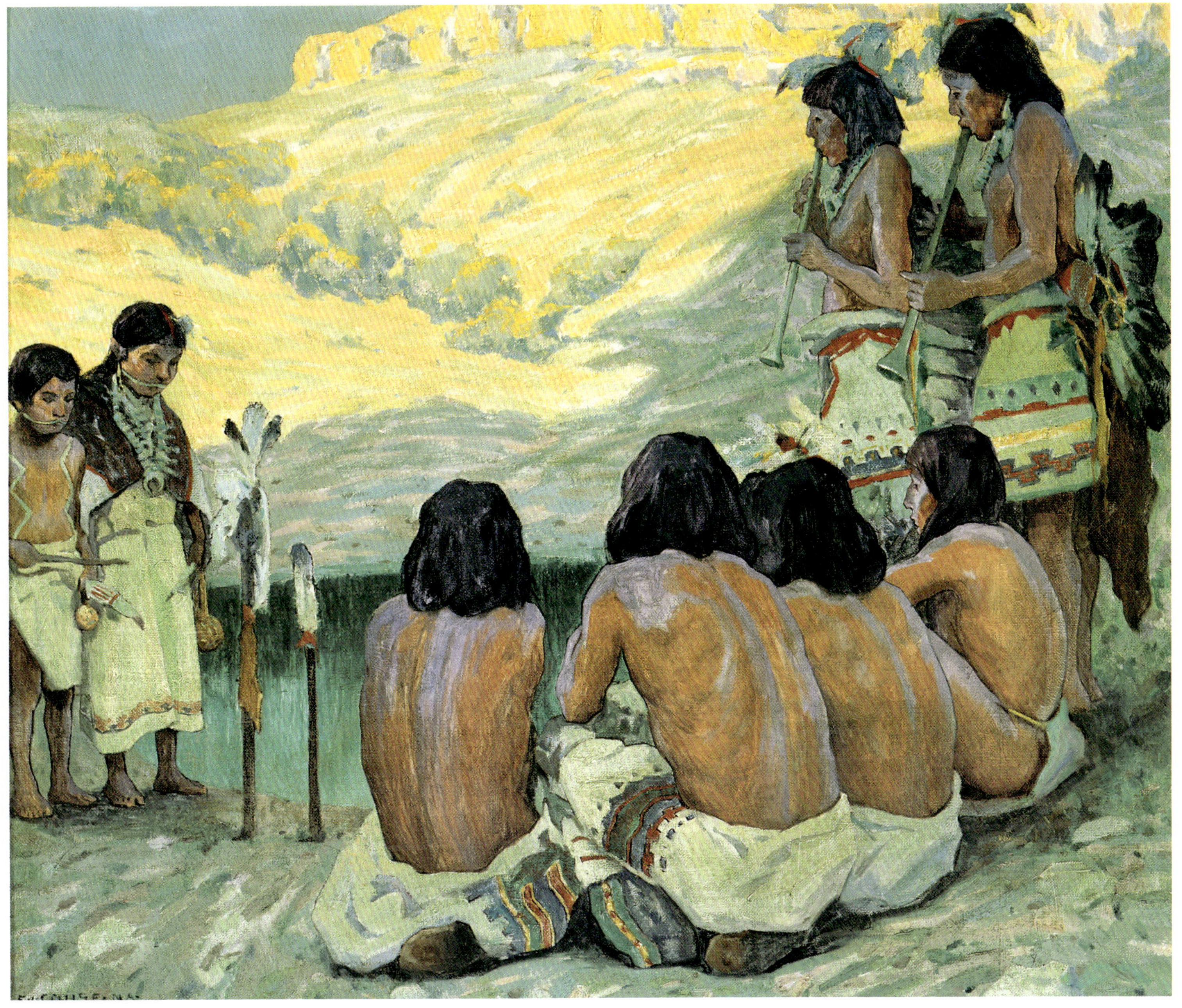

E. IRVING COUSE

(1866–1936)
The Flute Ceremony, 1922
oil on canvas
24 x 29 in. (61 x 73.7 cm)
Mr. and Mrs. Stewart Resnick

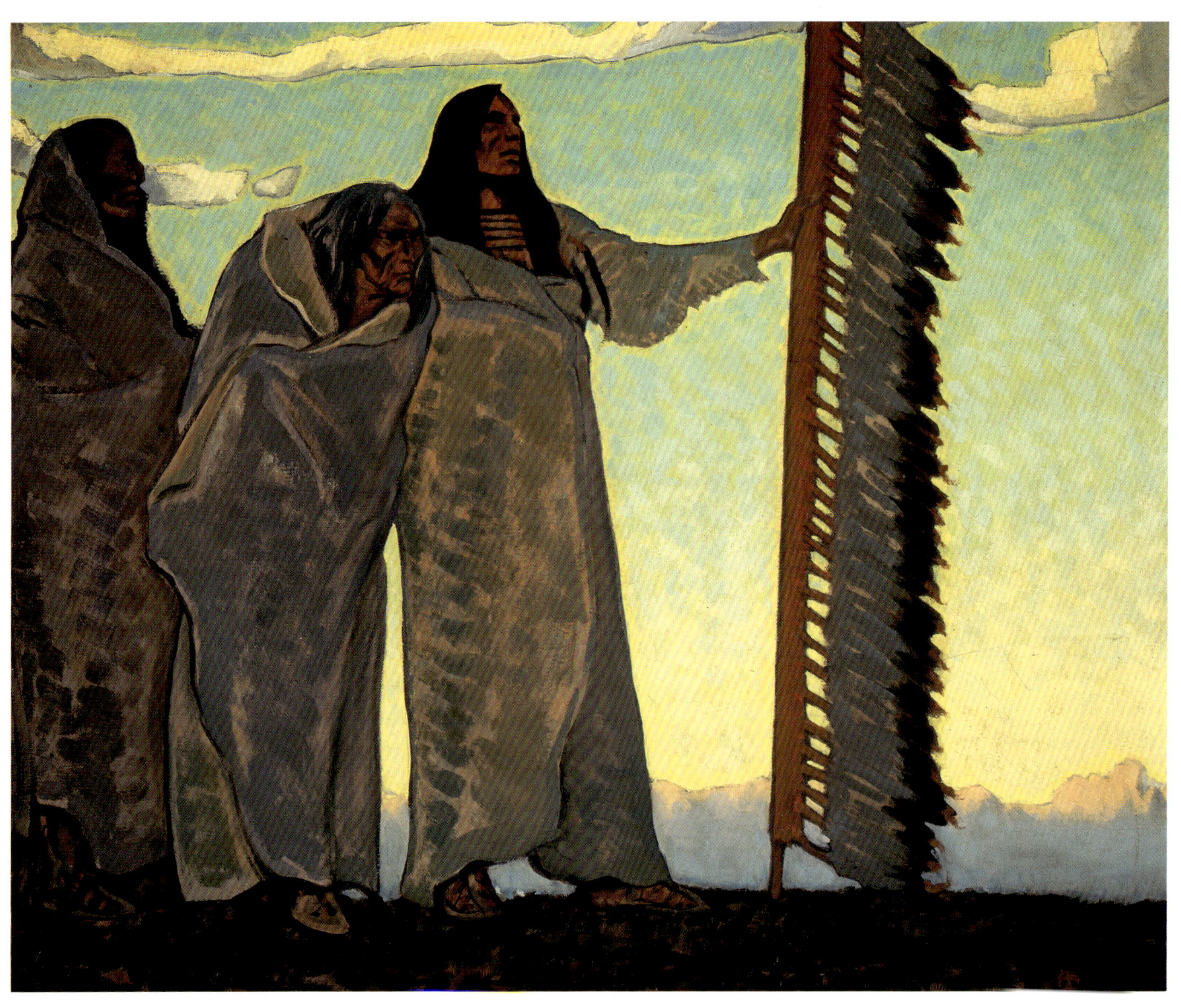

MAYNARD DIXON

(1875–1946)
The Ancients, 1922
oil on canvas
25 x 30⅜ in. (55.4 x 77.2 cm)
Mr. and Mrs. Stewart Resnick

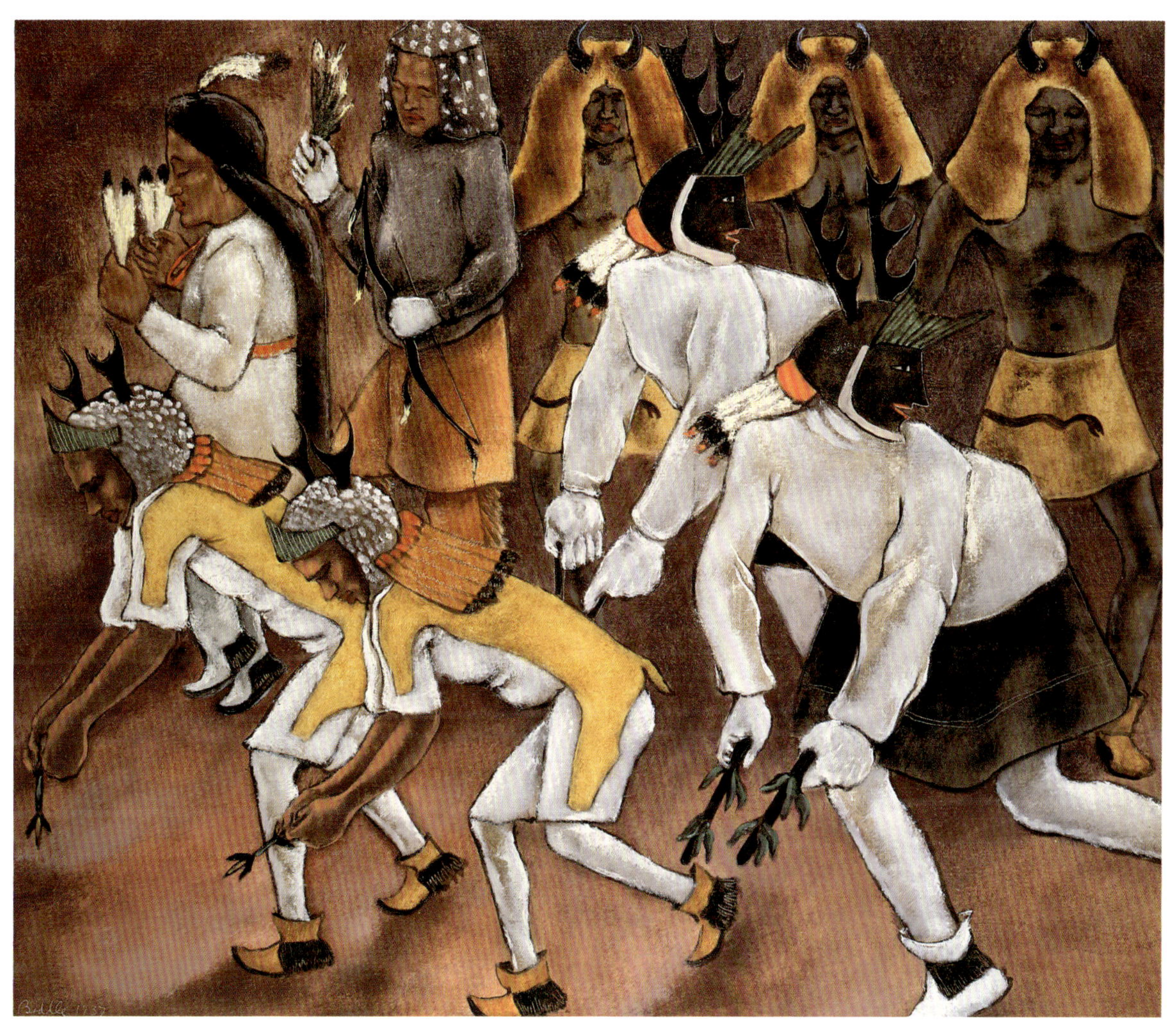

GEORGE BIDDLE

(1885–1973)
Indian Dance, No. 2, 1937
oil on canvas
25½ x 30 in. (64.8 x 76.2 cm)
Brenda and Gary Ruttenberg

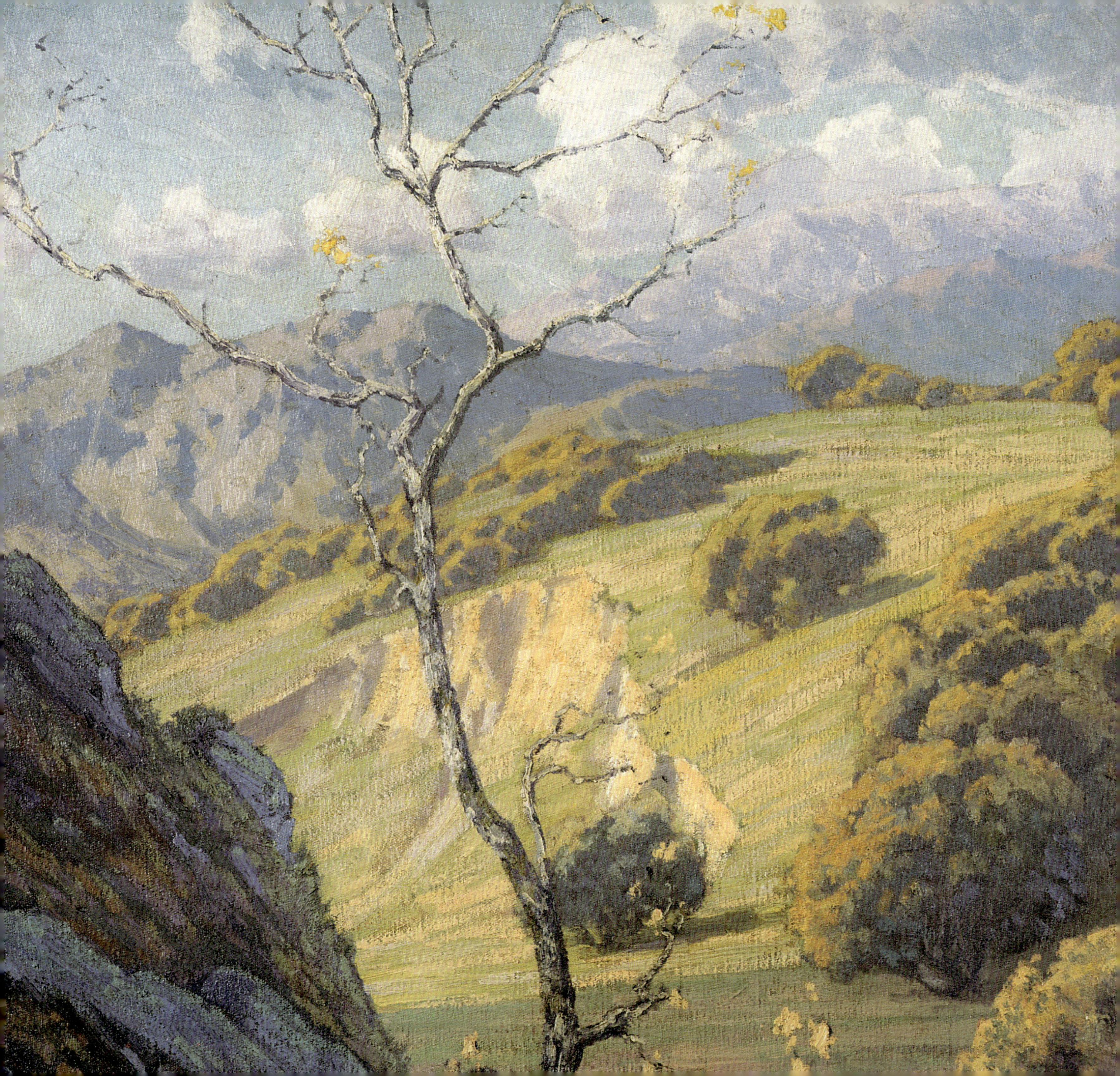

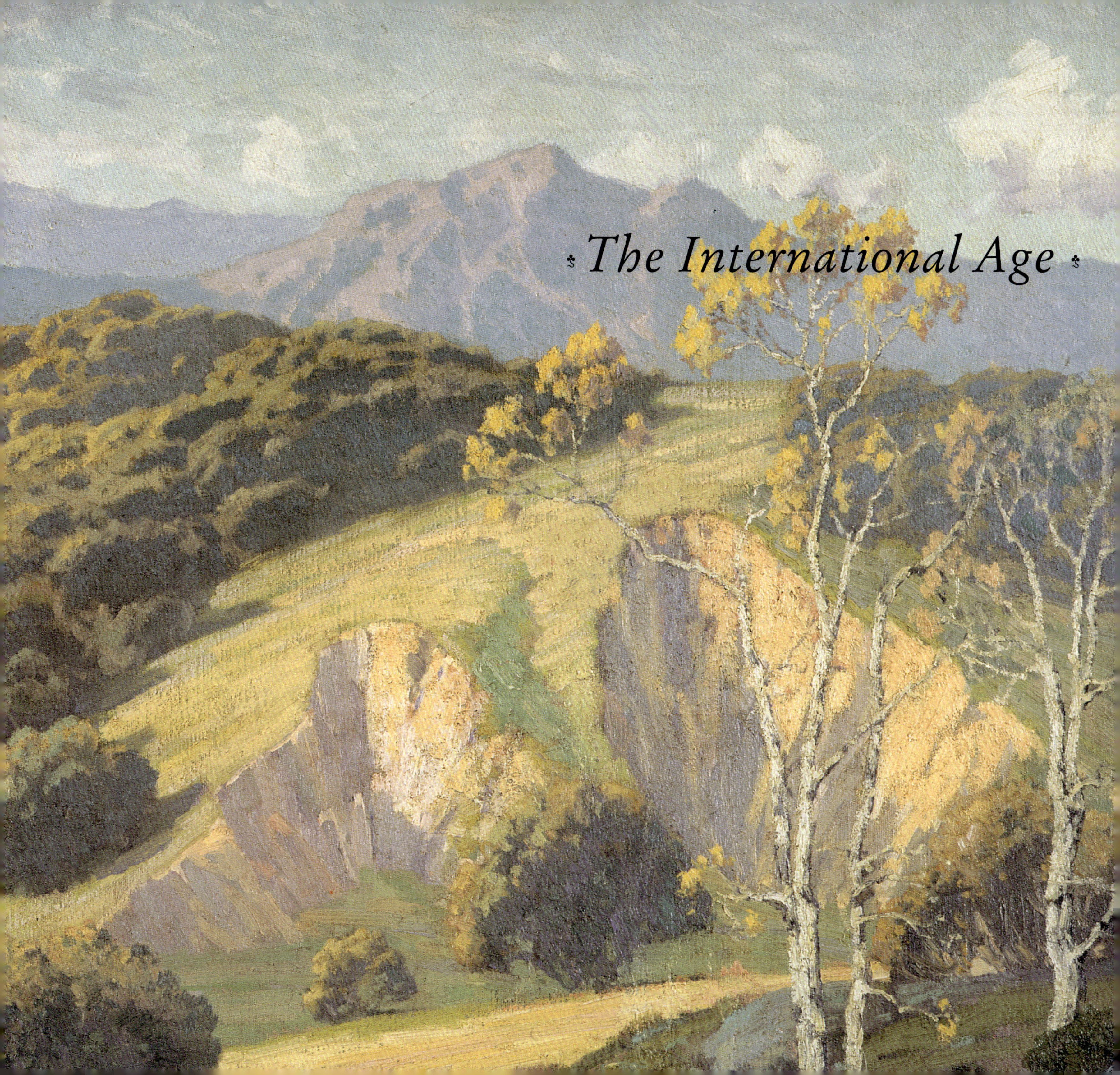

The International Age

After the civil war many wealthy American art patrons, desirous of developing a more worldly and sophisticated image, became captivated by European culture. American art, once favored because of its unique national sensibility, began to be viewed as somewhat parochial and naive. Moreover, because artistic training in the United States was still relatively rudimentary, many artists eager for more advanced instruction traveled to Europe to improve their skills.

European painting in the latter half of the nineteenth century was divided into warring factions. Academic painters extolled grandiose themes from history, composed in the studio. They followed strict training regimens and often used a technique that rendered their subjects in precise detail and with a highly polished finish. Avant-garde painters, on the other hand, rebelled against the rigid structure of academic painting and sought to portray contemporary life with more immediacy. Often they painted out-of-doors in what critics described as a sketchlike or "impressionist" style.

(previous pages)
MAURICE BRAUN
California Valley Farm
(detail)

In response to these divergent modes, American artists took different paths. Many elected to remain in Europe. Stimulated by the European craze for views of unfamiliar cultures, some painted scenes considered exotic by traditional standards. Peasant life, disappearing as a result of urbanization and industrialization, intrigued Charles Sprague Pearce and Thomas Hovenden. The mystique of North Africa and India was represented by Frederick Bridgman and Edwin Lord Weeks. African American artist Henry O. Tanner, seeking verisimilitude for his paintings of biblical themes, was drawn to the Holy Land and Mediterranean Africa.

Most American artists returned to the United States, eager to apply their

European training to American settings. Impressionism had fired the imagination of many, particularly those interested in depicting the landscape, and by 1900 it had become the dominant mode of artistic expression in the United States. Two of the best-known American impressionists, Maurice Prendergast and Childe Hassam, not only painted landscapes but incorporated figures in their scenes as well.

After the turn of the century, developments in transportation made coast-to-coast travel easier. Many artists found the golden glow of the California sun and the soft tonal qualities along the Pacific coastline an irresistible attraction. Guy Rose, who lived in Giverny for many years and was the first native-born Southern California artist to receive international attention, depicted the shoreline at Laguna Beach with a European-inspired impressionism. Other artists adopted a softer and more tonally harmonious approach. The subtly blended hues in Maurice Braun's *California Valley Farm* (c. 1920) exhibit this quality.

American art after the turn of the century could no longer be considered a poor cousin to its European relatives. As American artists came back to the United States, their high level of training and access to the most up-to-date European work allowed them to expand their artistic vocabulary and renew their vision of the American scene. ❦ —T.A.

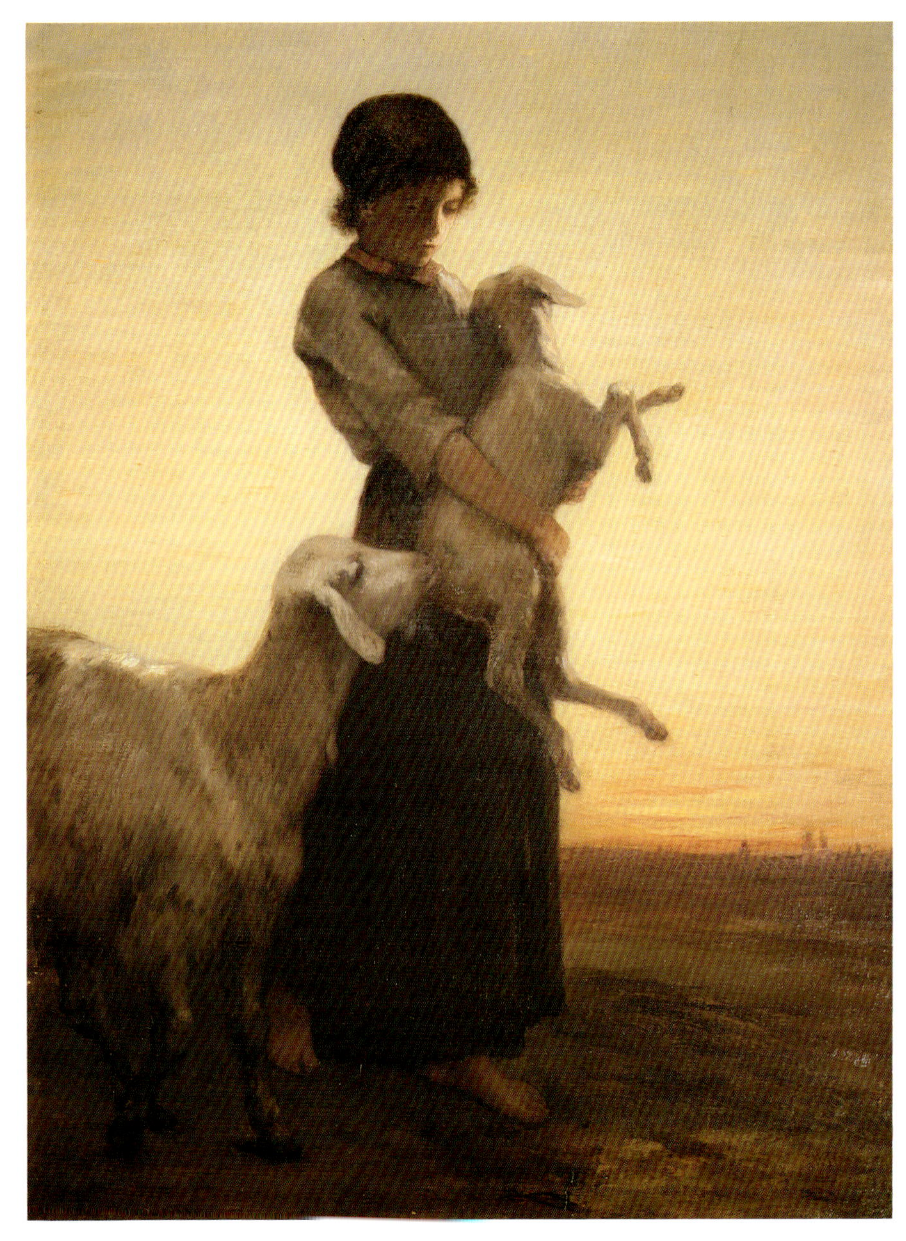

WILLIAM MORRIS HUNT

(1824–1879)
The Belated Kid, 1865
oil on canvas
23½ x 17½ in. (59.7 x 44.5 cm)
The Clark Family

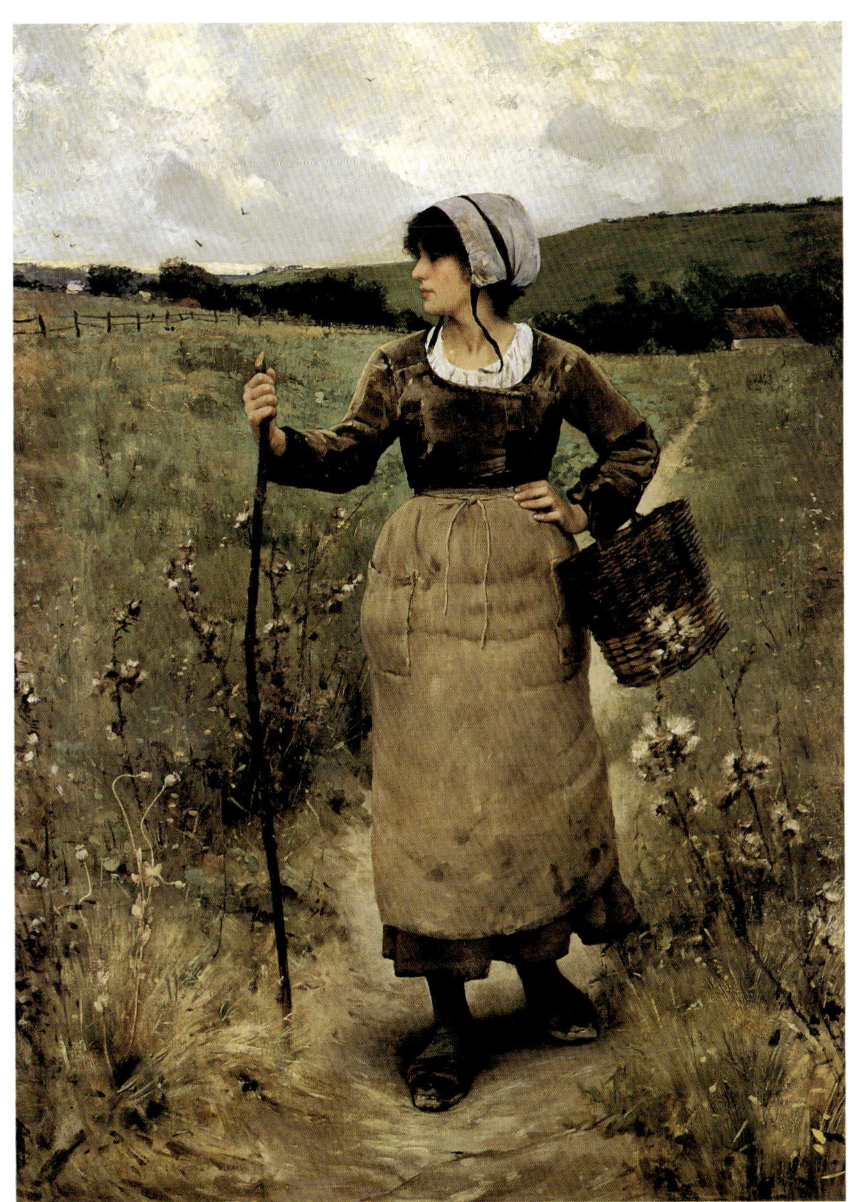

CHARLES SPRAGUE PEARCE

(1851–1914)
Across the Fields, c. 1884
oil on canvas
44½ x 32 in. (113 x 81.3 cm)
Mr. and Mrs. William Dana Lippman

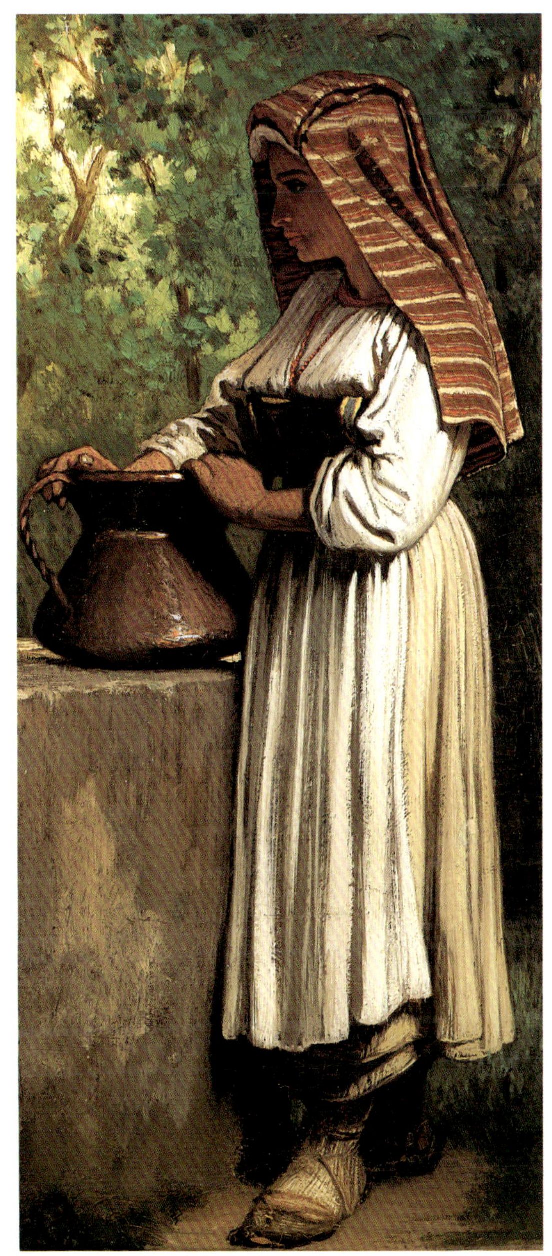

ELIHU VEDDER

(1836–1923)
Etruscan Girl, 1868
oil on canvas
10 x 5 in. (25.4 x 12.7 cm)
Mrs. Barbara Pauley Pagen

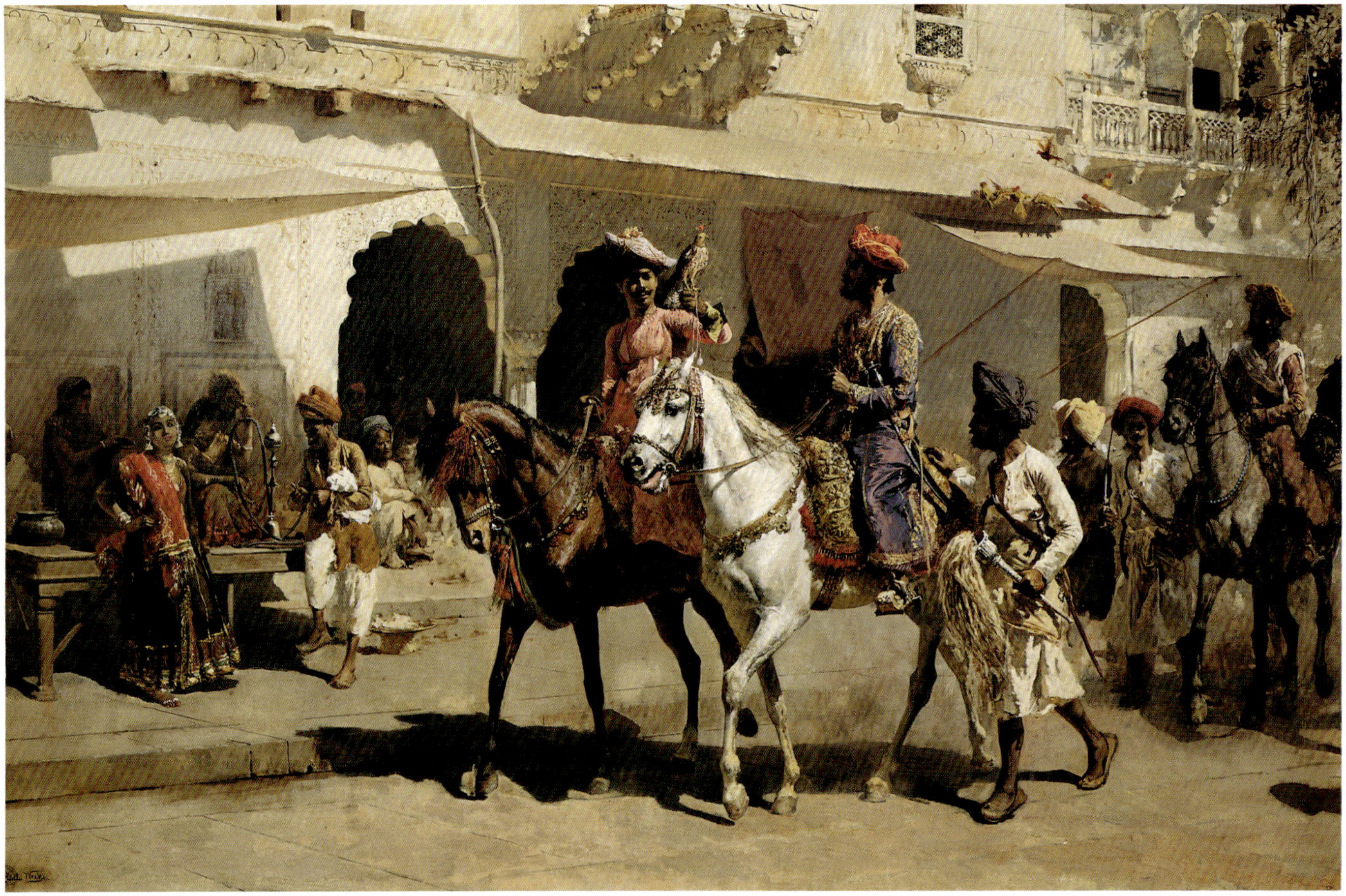

EDWIN LORD WEEKS

(1849–1903)
Start for the Hunt at Gwalior, c. 1884–94
oil on canvas
34 x 52¼ in. (86.4 x 132.7 cm)
Patricia and Richard Anawalt

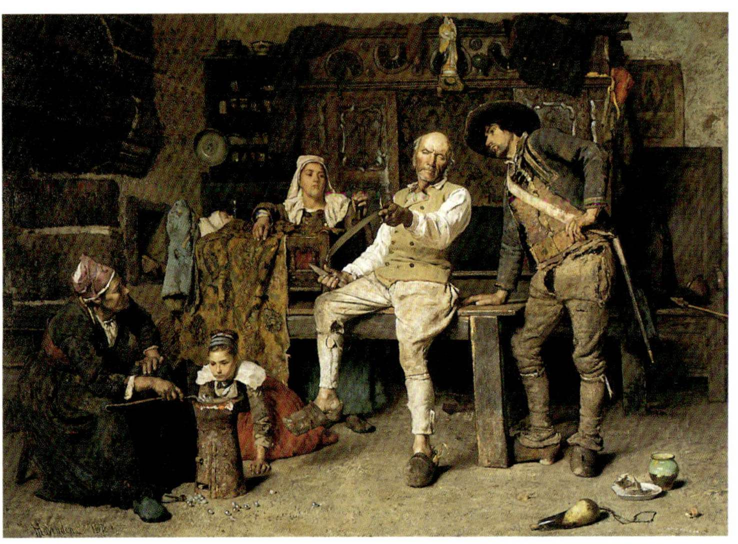

THOMAS HOVENDEN

(1840–1895)
A Breton Interior (A Vendean Volunteer), 1878
oil on canvas
38¼ x 54 in. (97.2 x 137.2 cm)
Dr. and Mrs. Robert M. Carroll

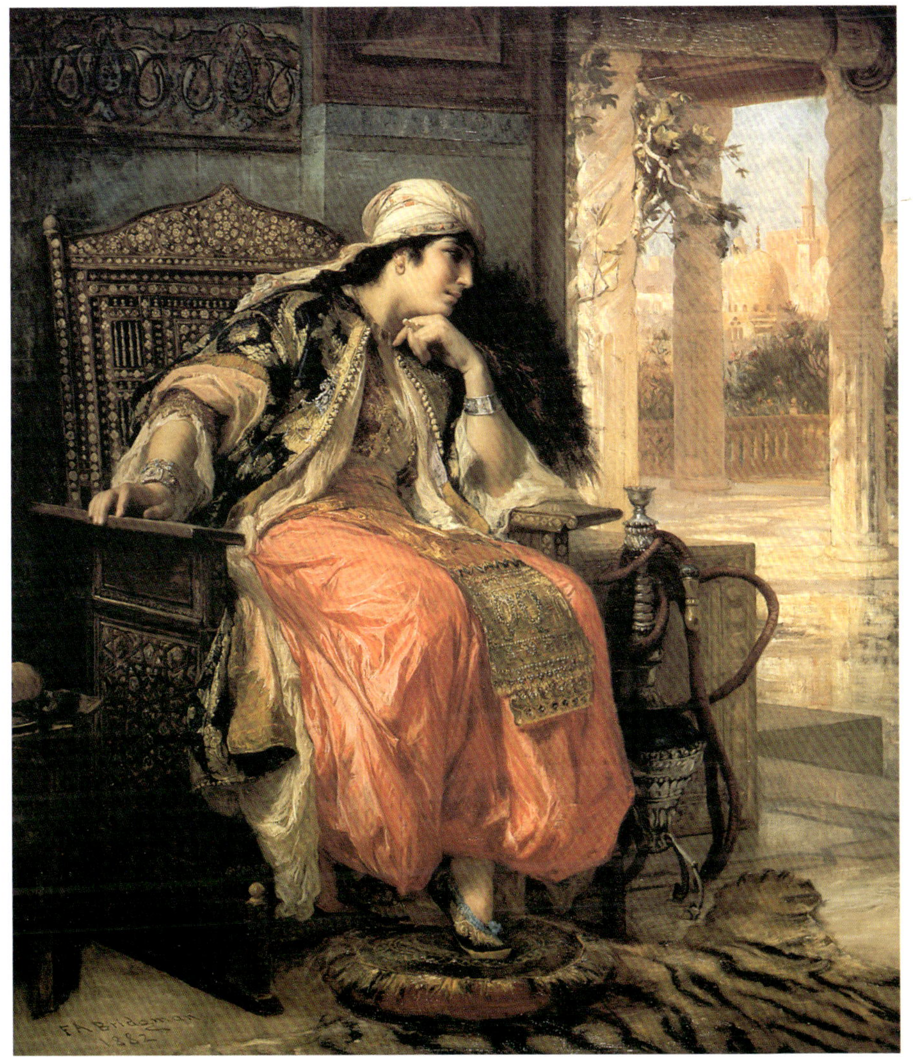

FREDERICK A. BRIDGMAN

(1847–1928)
The Favorite, 1882
oil on canvas
49 x 43 in. (124.5 x 109.2 cm)
Patricia and Richard Anawalt

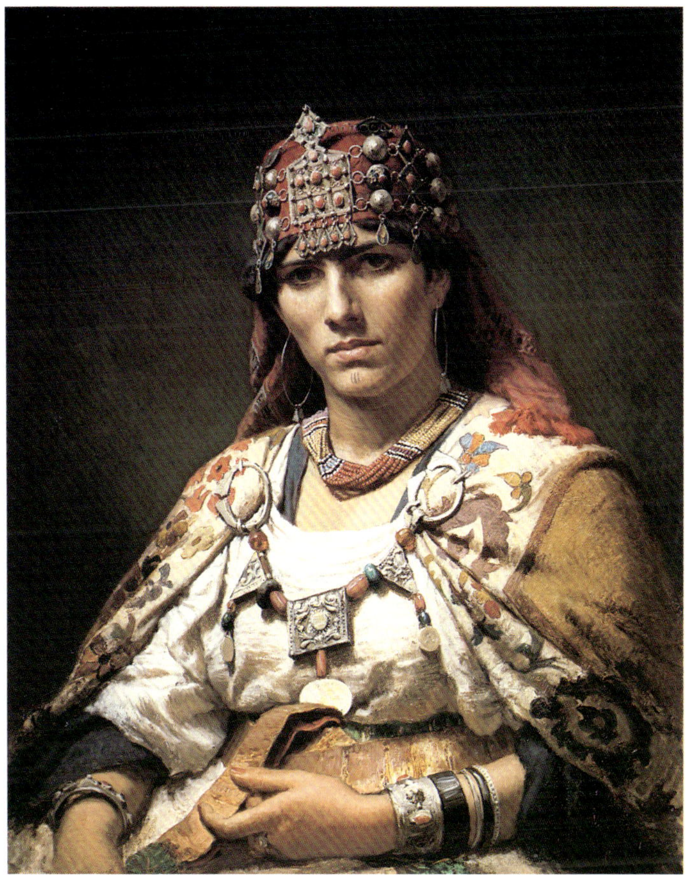

FREDERICK A. BRIDGMAN

(1847–1928)
Aicha, Woman of the Kabylia Mountains, 1875
oil on canvas
28½ x 23 in. (72.4 x 58.4 cm)
Mr. and Mrs. Robert Bruce Tebbe

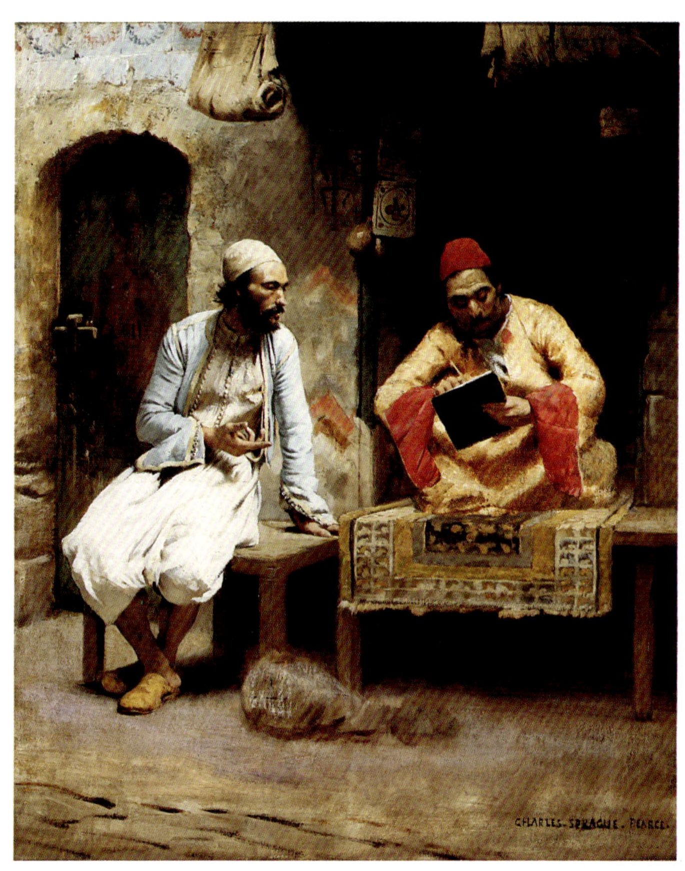

CHARLES SPRAGUE PEARCE

(1851–1914)
The Letter, c. 1874–82
oil on canvas
21⅝ x 17⅝ in. (54.9 x 44.8 cm)
Mr. and Mrs. Arnold C. Kirkeby

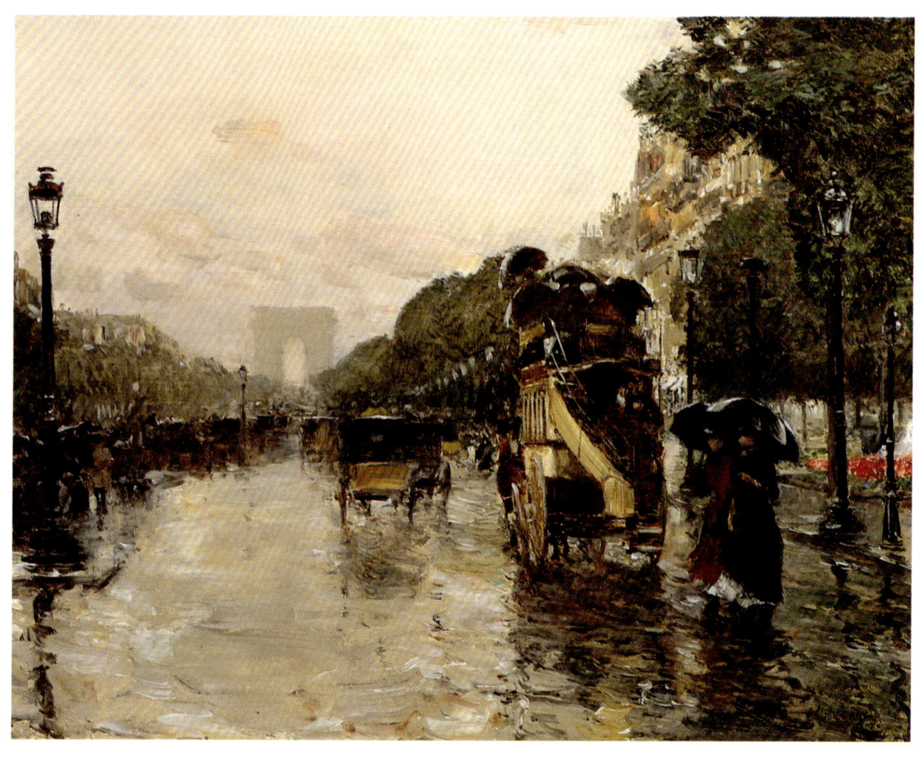

CHILDE HASSAM

(1859–1935)
Champs Elysées, Paris, 1889
oil on canvas
12¼ x 16 in. (31.1 x 40.6 cm)
private collection,
courtesy of Guggenheim, Asher Associates Inc.

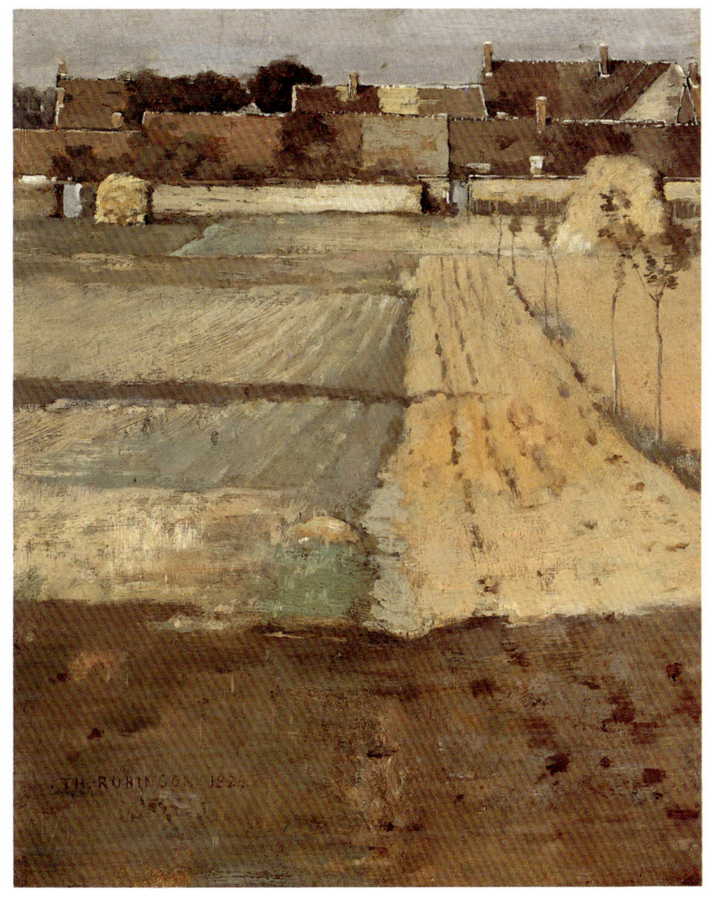

THEODORE ROBINSON

(1852–1896)
Barbizon, 1884
oil on canvas
16 x 12¾ in. (40.6 x 32.4 cm)
Jean and Samuel Sapin

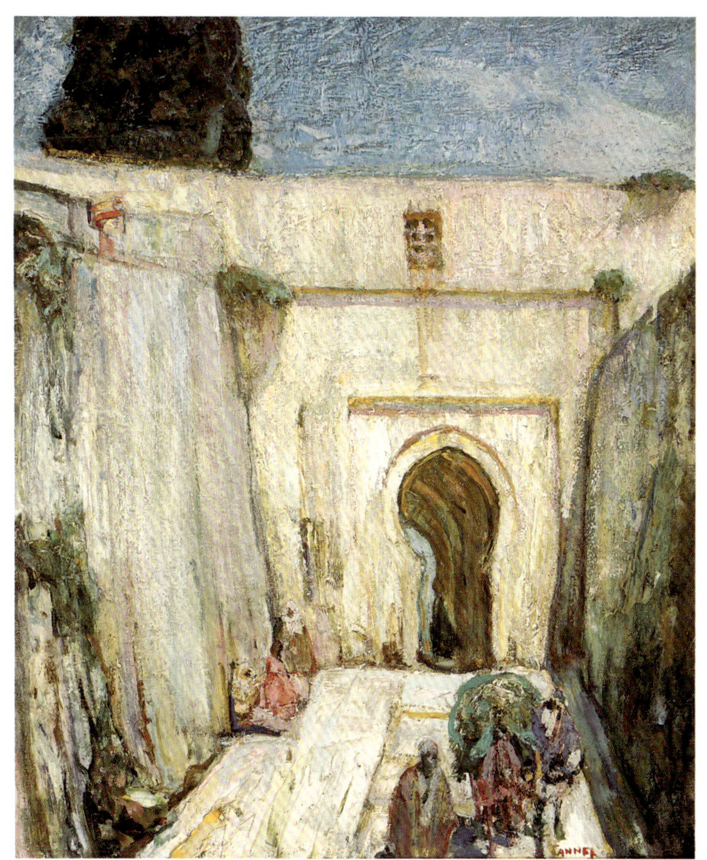

HENRY O. TANNER

(1859–1937)
Midday Tangiers, c. 1915
oil on canvas
24 x 20 in. (61 x 50.8 cm)
private collection

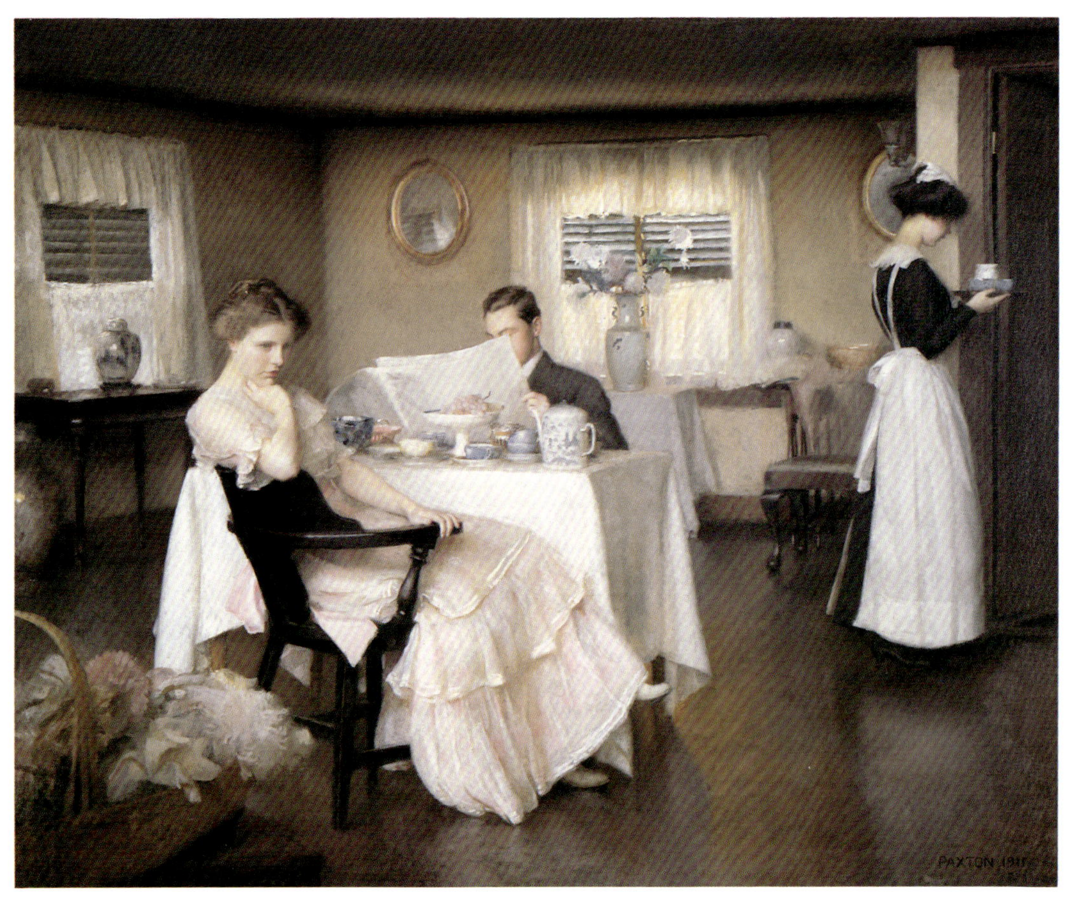

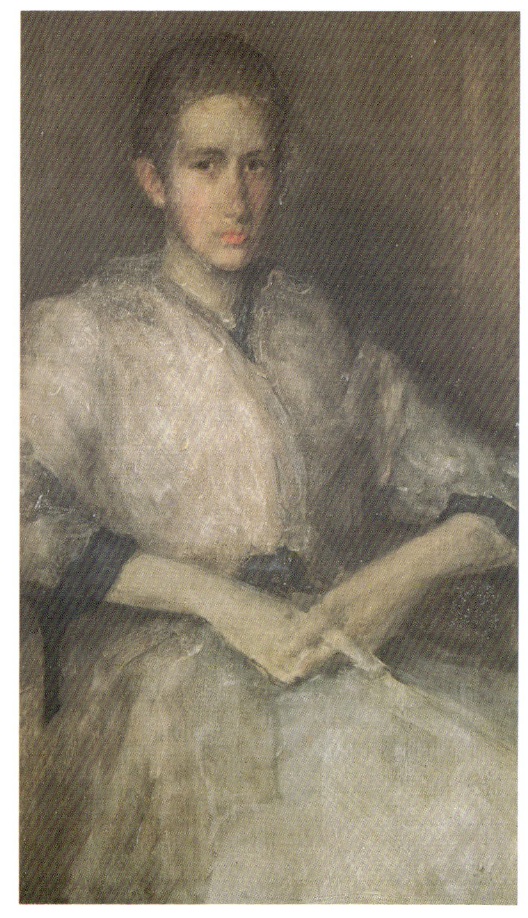

WILLIAM PAXTON

(1869–1941)
The Breakfast, 1911
oil on canvas
28 x 34 in. (71.1 x 86.4 cm)
Ted and Carole Slavin

JAMES A. M. WHISTLER

(1834–1903)
Portrait of Ellen Sturgis Hooper, 1890
oil on wood panel
20⅛ x 12⅛ in. (51.1 x 30.8 cm)
The Clark Family

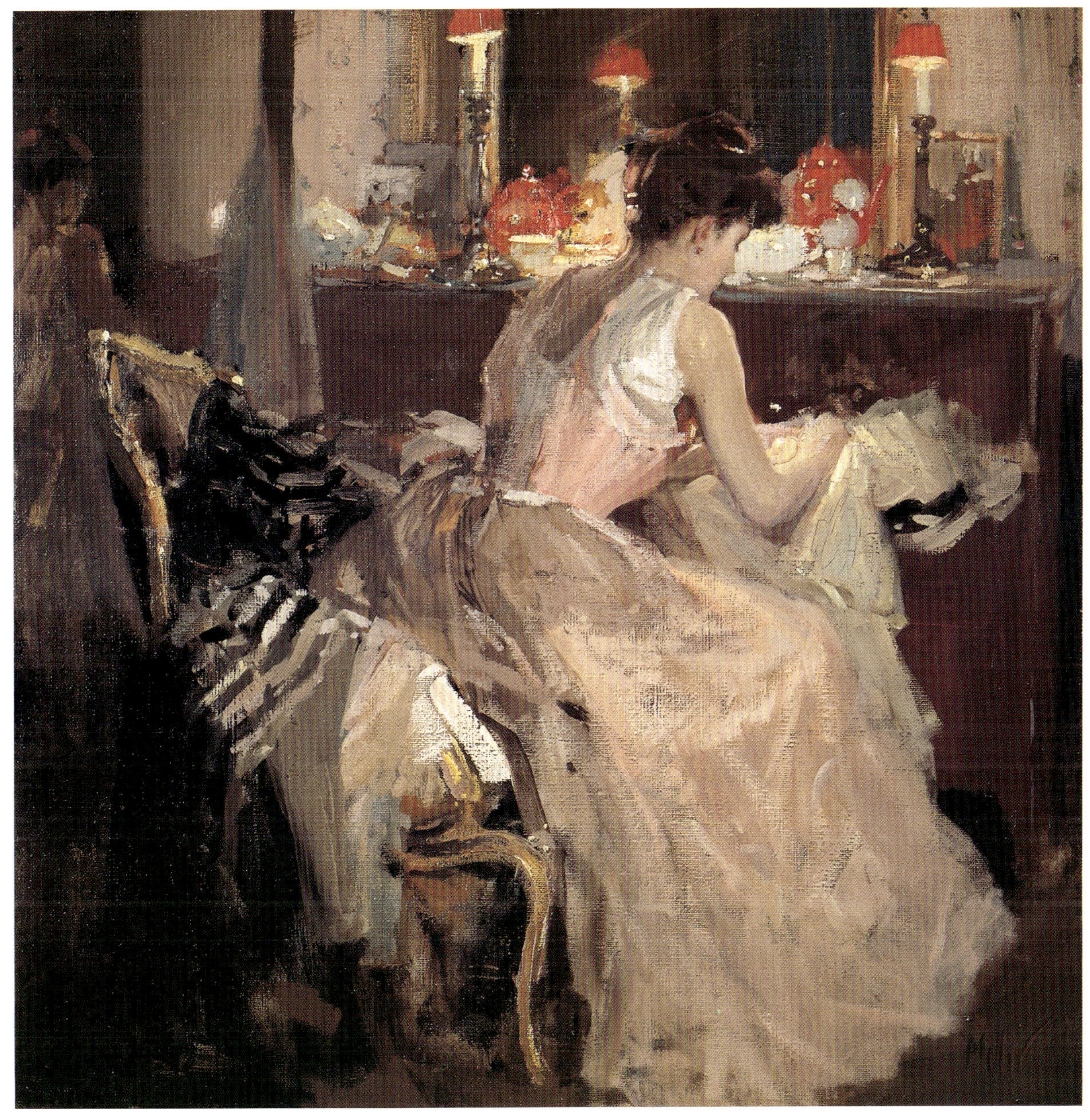

RICHARD MILLER

(1875–1943)
Sewing by Lamplight, 1904
oil on canvas
24 x 24 in. (61 x 61 cm)
Iris and B. Gerald Cantor

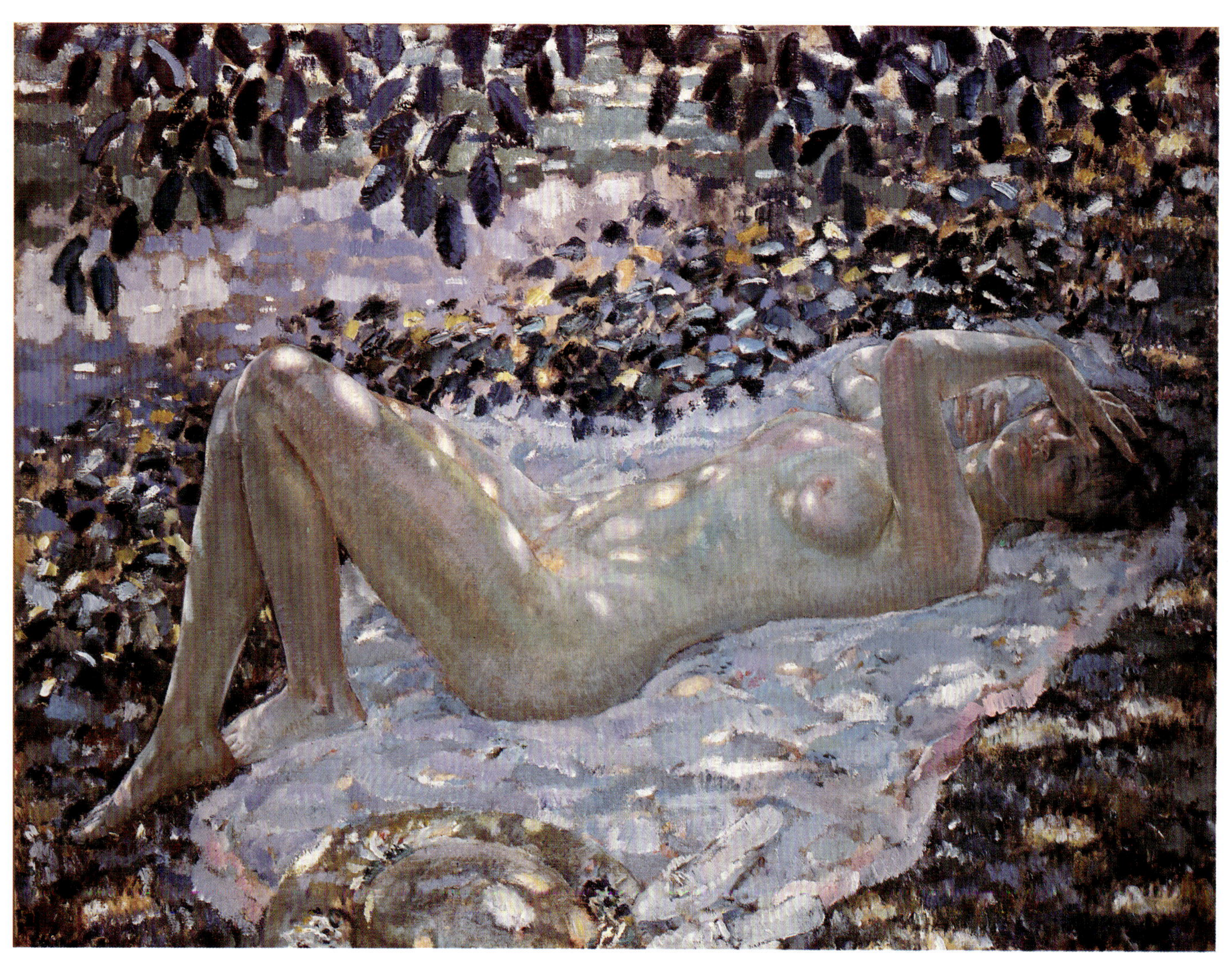

FREDERICK FRIESEKE

(1874–1939)
Nude in Dappled Sunlight, 1915
oil on canvas
38 x 51⅛ in. (66 x 81.3 cm)
private collection

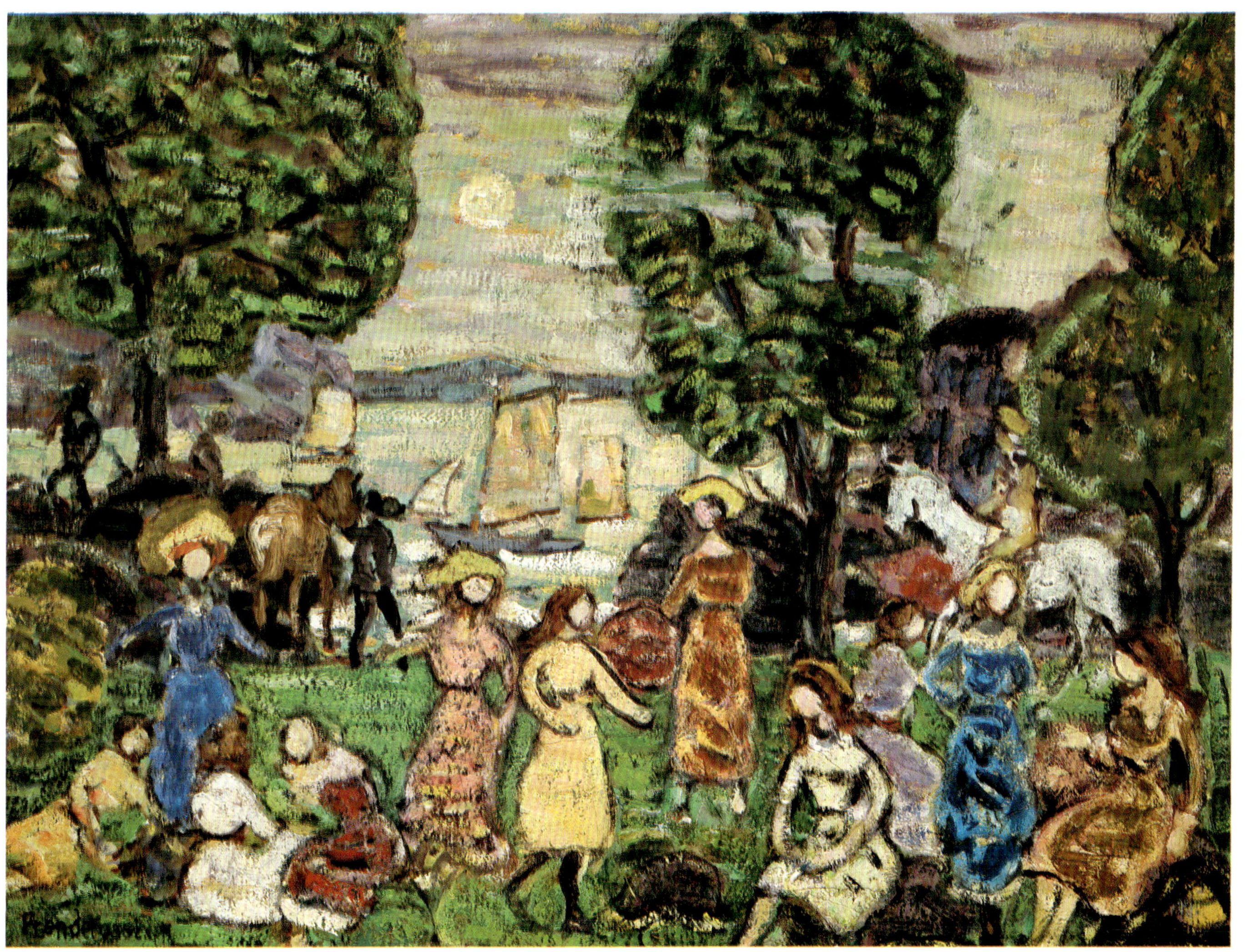

MAURICE PRENDERGAST

(1858–1924)
Crepuscule, 1918–23
oil on canvas
21 x 27 in. (53.3 x 68.6 cm)
Nancy Daly

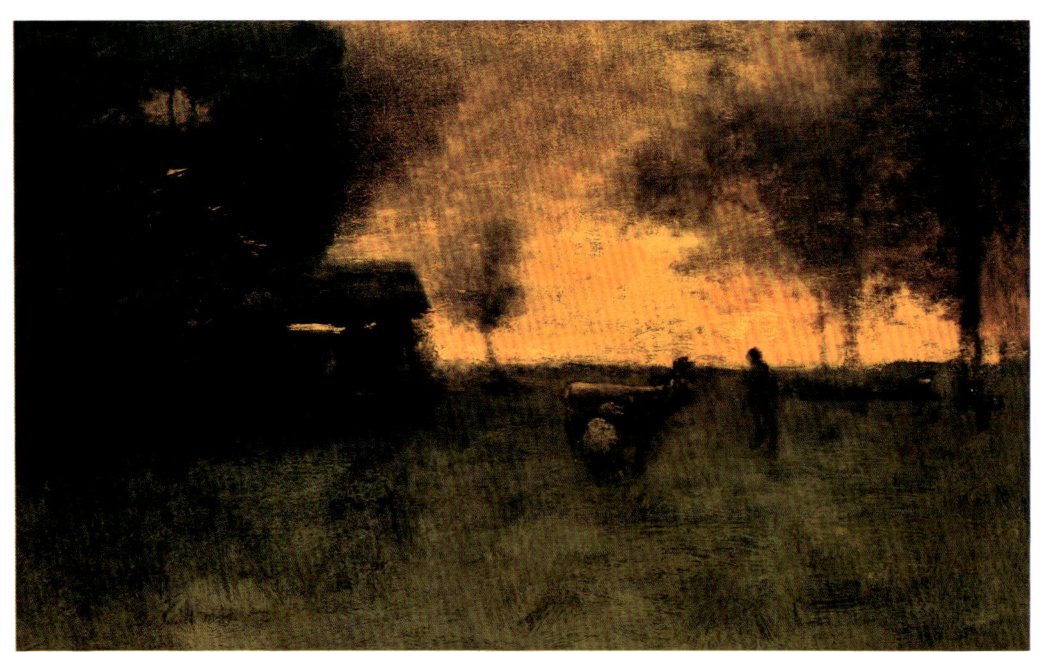

GEORGE INNESS

(1825–1894)
Sunset, Milking Time, Montclair, 1889
oil on canvas
(21⅞ x 36⅛ in. (55.6 x 91.8 cm)
James and Ruth Gumbiner

RALPH A. BLAKELOCK

(1847–1919)
Sunset Silhouette, n.d.
oil on canvas
16 x 24 in. (40.6 x 61 cm)
Camilla Chandler Frost

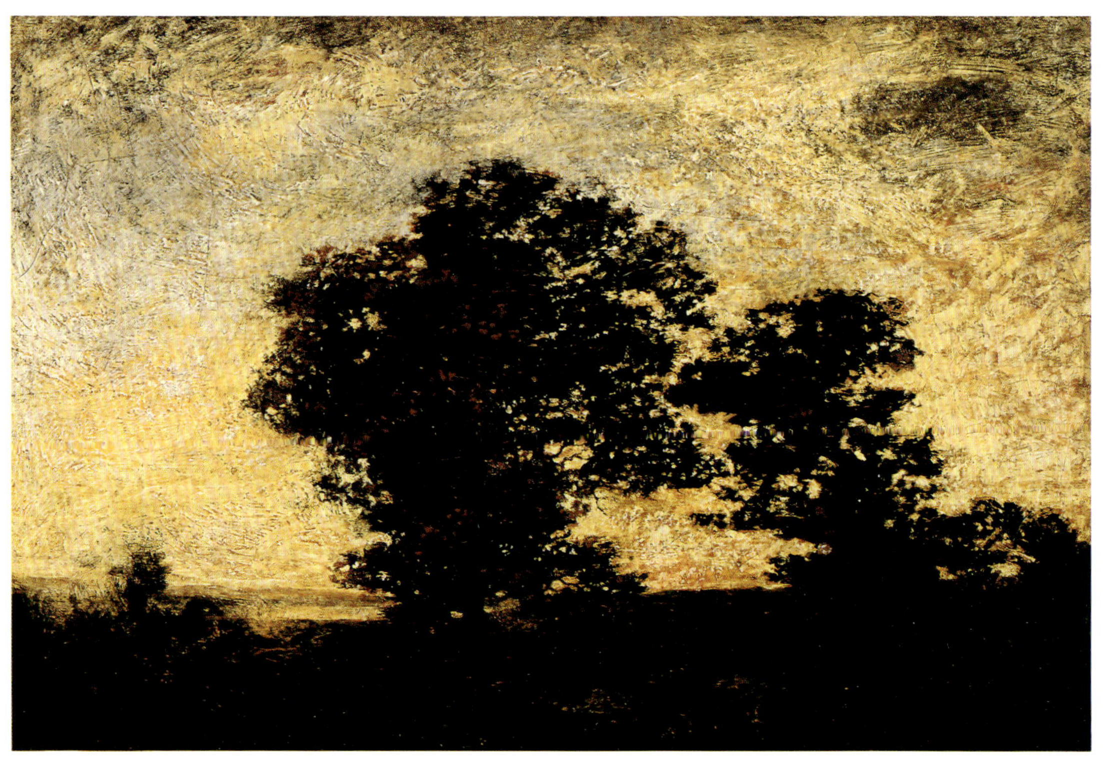

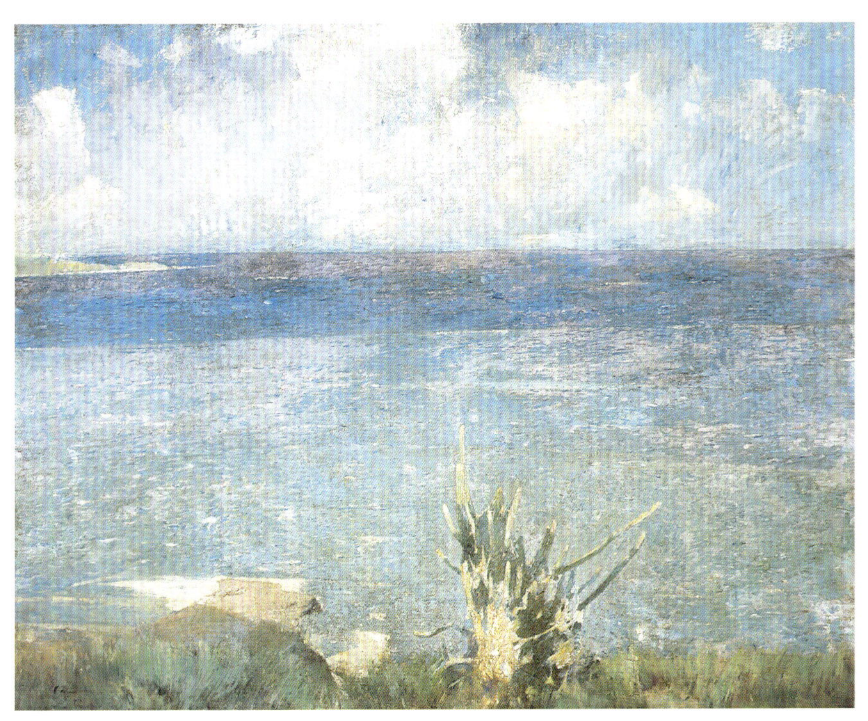

EMIL CARLSEN

(1853–1932)
The Caribbean, 1913
oil on canvas
40 x 50 in. (101.6 x 127 cm)
Bobbi and Walter Zifkin

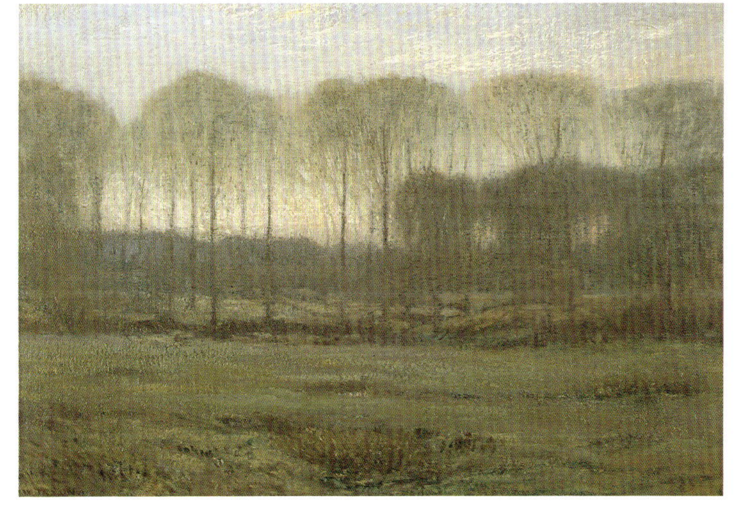

DWIGHT TRYON

(1849–1925)
Early Morning
(Dawn —Early Spring), by 1903
oil on canvas
20 x 30 in. (50.8 x 76.2 cm)
The Clark Family

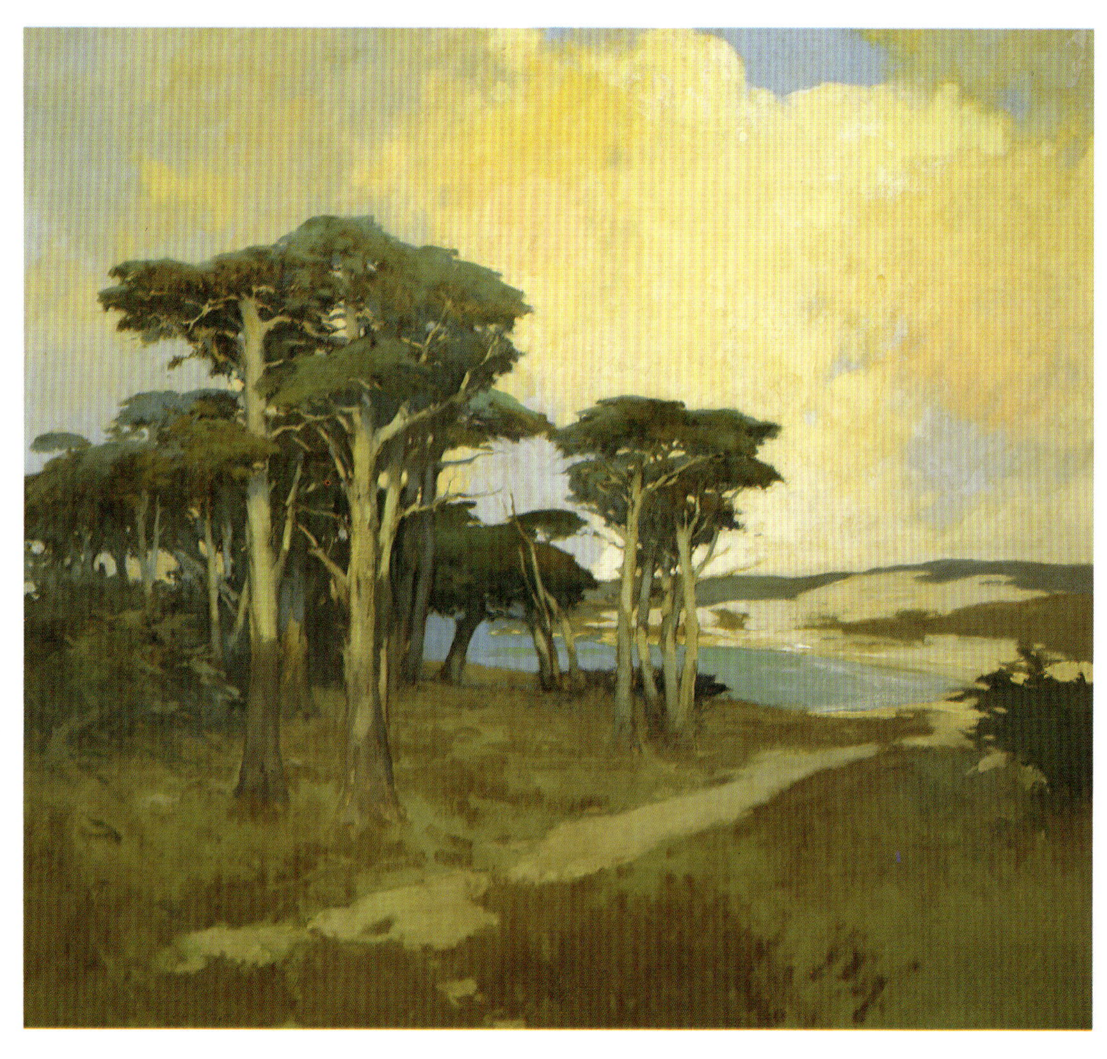

ARTHUR MATHEWS

(1860–1945)
Monterey Cypress, c. 1930
oil on canvas
42 x 46 in. (106.7 x 116.8 cm)
Nancy Daly

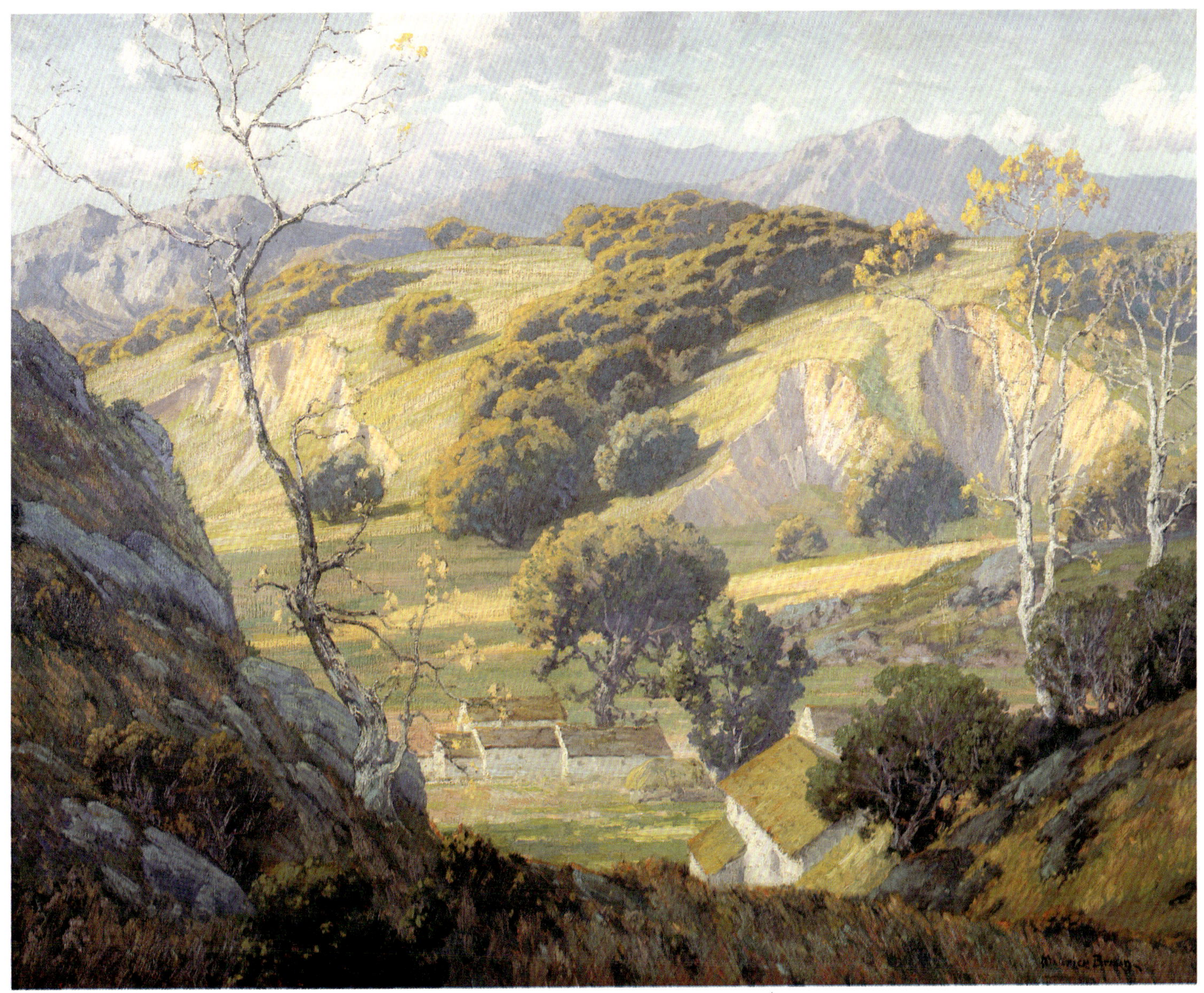

MAURICE BRAUN

(1877–1941)
California Valley Farm, c. 1920
oil on canvas
40 x 50 in. (101.6 x 127 cm)
Joseph L. Moure

GUY ROSE

(1867–1925)
The Shoreline, c. 1914–21
oil on canvas
23 x 29 in. (58.4 x 73.7 cm)
lent anonymously

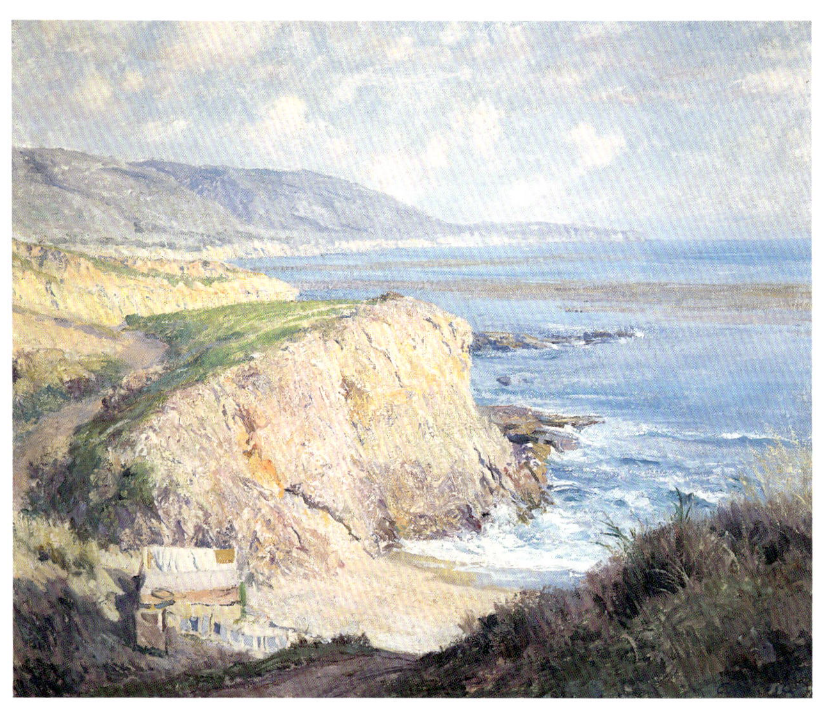

GRANVILLE REDMOND

(1871–1935)
Poppy Field with Oaks and Lupines, late 1910s–20s
oil on canvas
40 x 60 in. (101.6 x 152.4 cm)
private collection

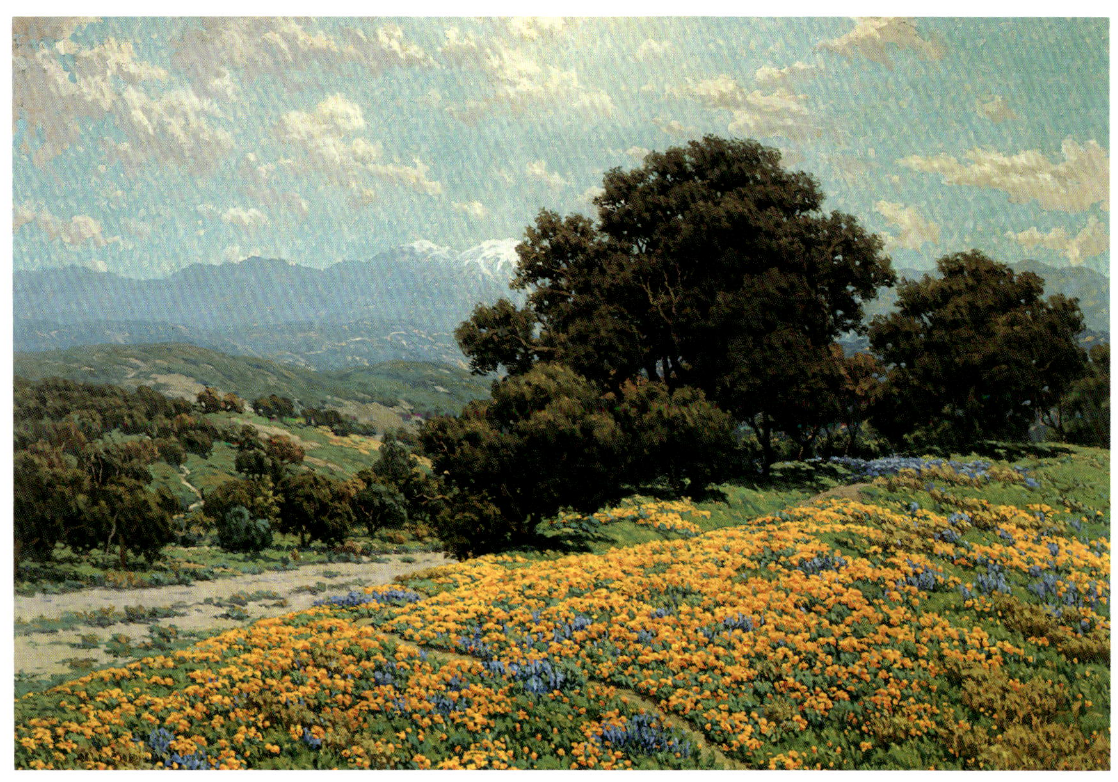

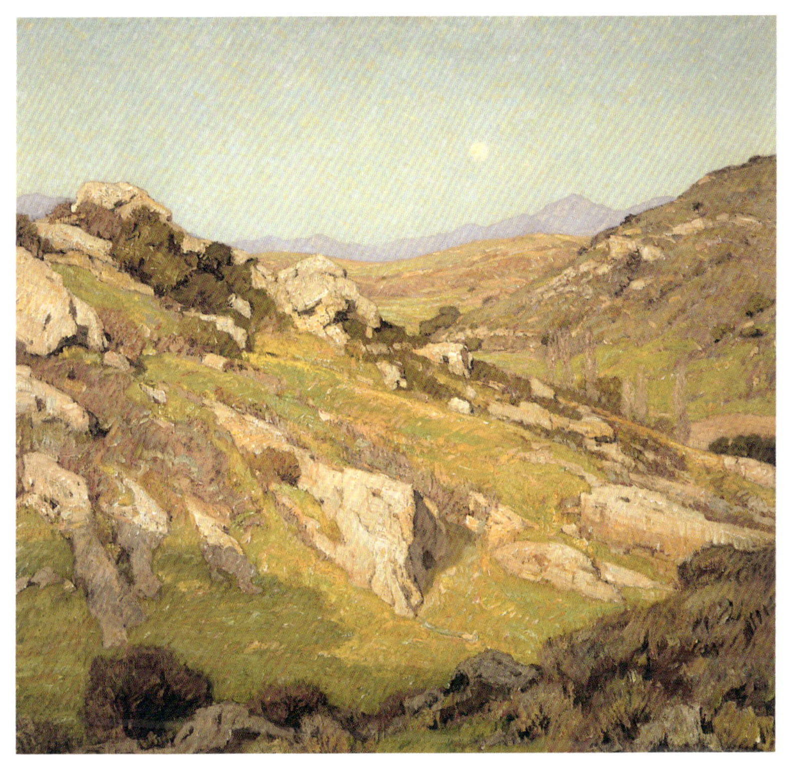

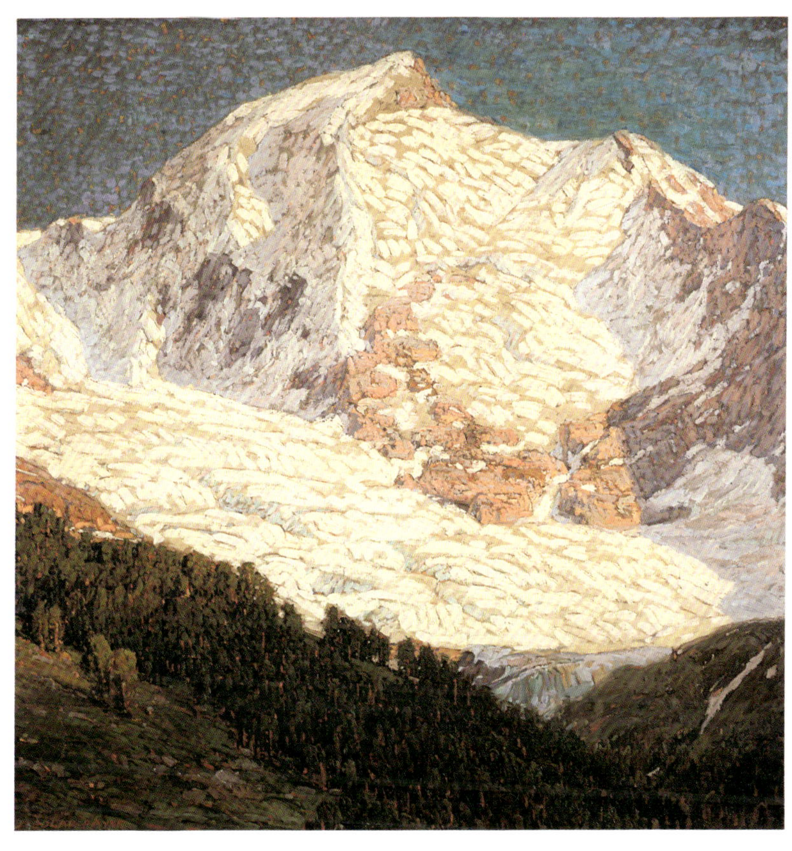

WILLIAM WENDT

(1865–1946)
There Is No Solitude, Even in Nature, 1906
oil on canvas
34 x 36 in. (86.4 x 91.4 cm)
Mrs. Joan Irvine Smith

EDGAR ALWYN PAYNE

(1882–1947)
The Great White Peak, No. 2, 1924
oil on canvas
62 x 62 in. (157.5 x 157.5 cm)
James and Linda Ries,
promised gift to the
Los Angeles County Museum of Art

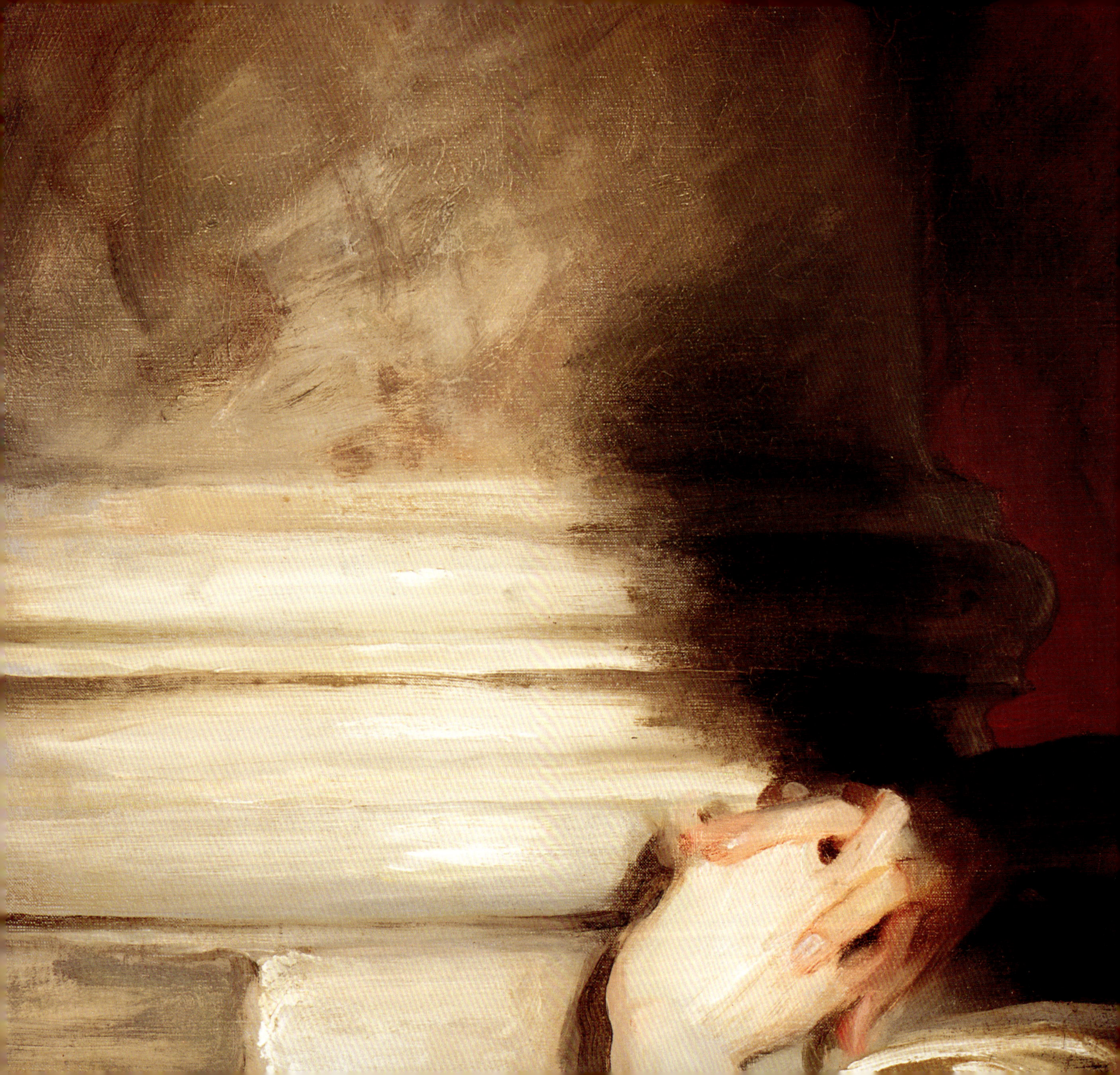

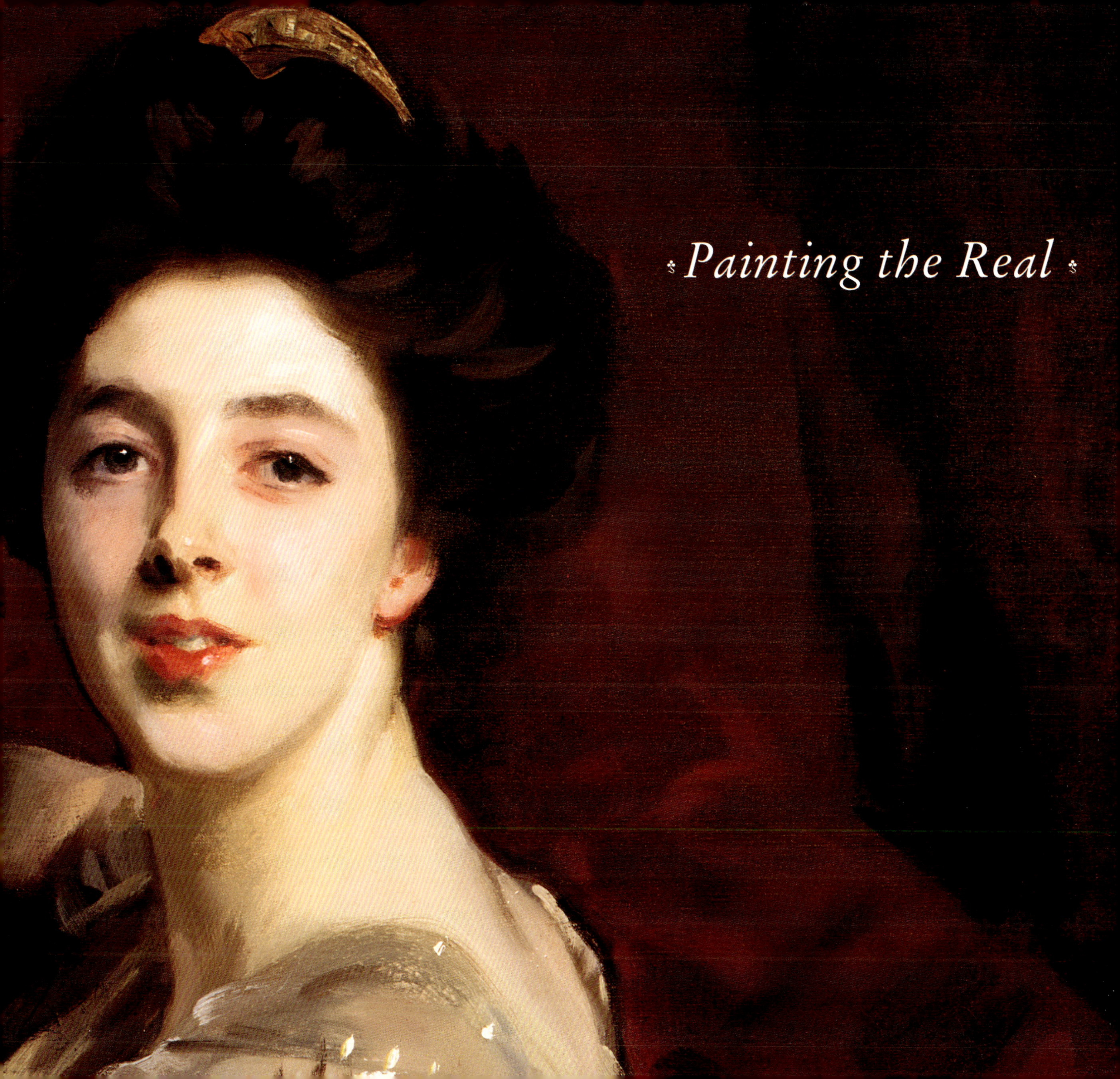
Painting the Real

Realism is a paradoxical term that takes on different meanings in different circumstances. It often refers to paintings that endeavor to present objective and impartial views of people, places, and things in an almost scientific fashion. Realist artists in this sense employ an exacting method of drawing or painting to carefully delineate the precise details of their subjects. Trompe l'oeil ("fool the eye") painting lies at the extreme end of the realist spectrum. William Harnett's *Mr. Hulings' Rack Picture* (1888) playfully teases the viewer; the objects in the painting are so meticulously rendered that they can almost be taken for actual objects.

(previous pages)
JOHN SINGER SARGENT
Portrait of Izme Vickers
(detail)

Realism is sometimes thought to reflect a particularly American pragmatic attitude, and Thomas Eakins is often considered the quintessential American realist. Primarily known for his portraits, he uncompromisingly captured the character of his sitters with a truthfulness frequently thought unflattering by them. In his *Portrait of Mrs. Kern Dodge* (1904) Eakins pictured a woman whose life experience and personality seem to vividly emerge from the canvas.

In contrast to such stern and somber realist paintings are the canvases of the American expatriate artists John Singer Sargent and James A. M. Whistler, who painted members of an elegant, cosmopolitan culture. Working in France, England, and the United States, Sargent captured the beauty and charm of his prestigious sitters in a manner popular with upper-class society. Whistler, adopting the style of the English Aesthetic Movement, broke new ground in depicting his subjects as a part of a larger artistic statement. His insistence on a formal harmony among his colors and shapes resulted in work that was as attuned to compositional demands as to its subject matter.

Another form of realism was influenced by the French avant-garde movement begun by Gustave Courbet. These realists eschewed historical or idealized motifs that could not be seen in the contemporary world. Such artists often painted scenes not previously considered suitable for artistic portrayal because of their mundane nature. A group of New York–based artists known as the ashcan school aggressively depicted urban life as experienced by its poorer citizens. Robert Henri and William Glackens rendered the inhabitants and locales of New York with a bravura and honesty that suggests the no-nonsense attitude of city life.

The tradition of realism evident in paintings by the ashcan school was accelerated by social problems following the end of World War I and the economic hardships of the 1930s. Jared French, William Gropper, and other social realists took a critical view of American political life and economic conditions during this era. Pointing to harsh dichotomies between social classes, ethnic groups, and political ideologies, these artists made barbed comments upon contemporary life and left a legacy of social criticism that forms another strain of American realism. ⚘ –T.A.

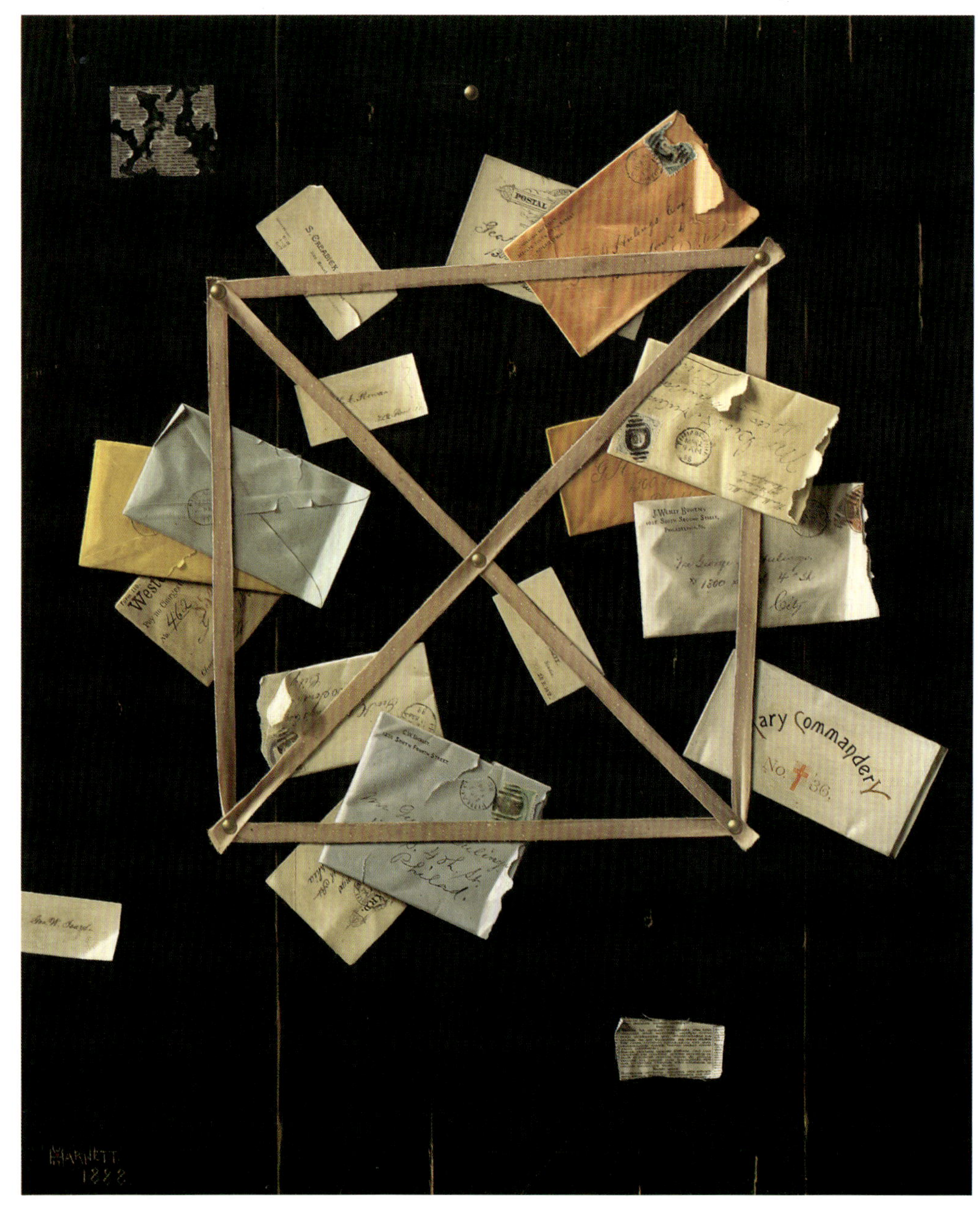

WILLIAM MICHAEL HARNETT

(1848–1892)
Mr. Hulings' Rack Picture, 1888
oil on canvas
30 x 25 in. (76.2 x 63.5 cm)
Jo Ann and Julian Ganz Jr.

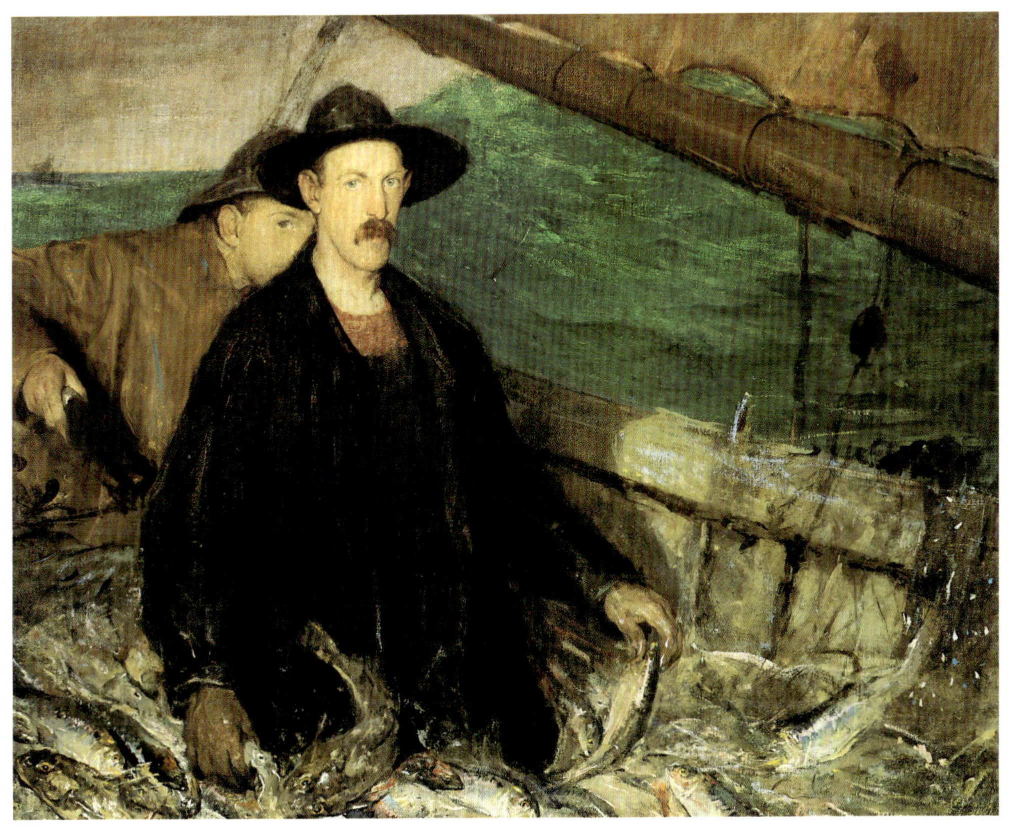

CHARLES HAWTHORNE

(1872–1930)
Return from the Sea, 1909
oil on canvas
48 ⅛ x 60⅝ in. (122.2 x 154 cm)
Sidney and Diana Avery Trust

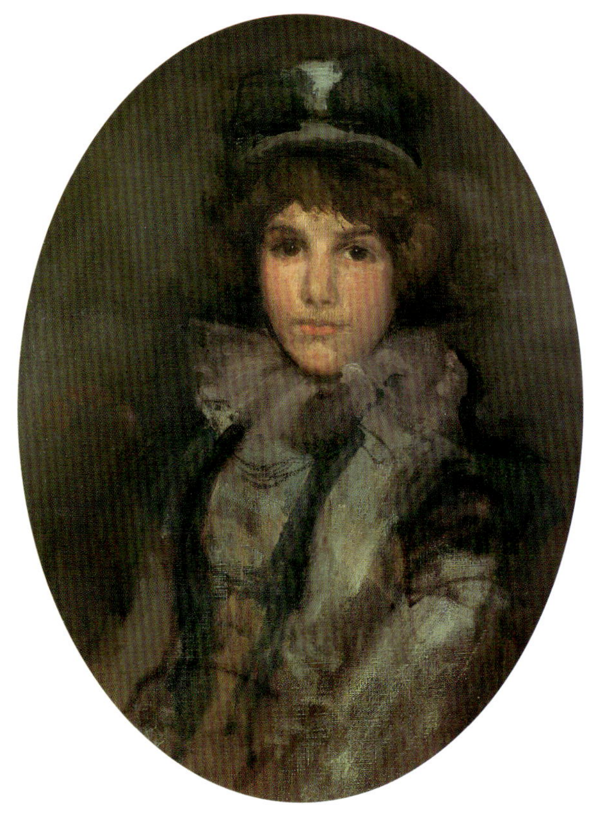

JAMES A. M. WHISTLER

(1834–1903)
Blue and Coral: The Little Blue Bonnet, 1898
oil on canvas
23 x 18 in. (58.4 x 45.7 cm)
John and Gail Liebes

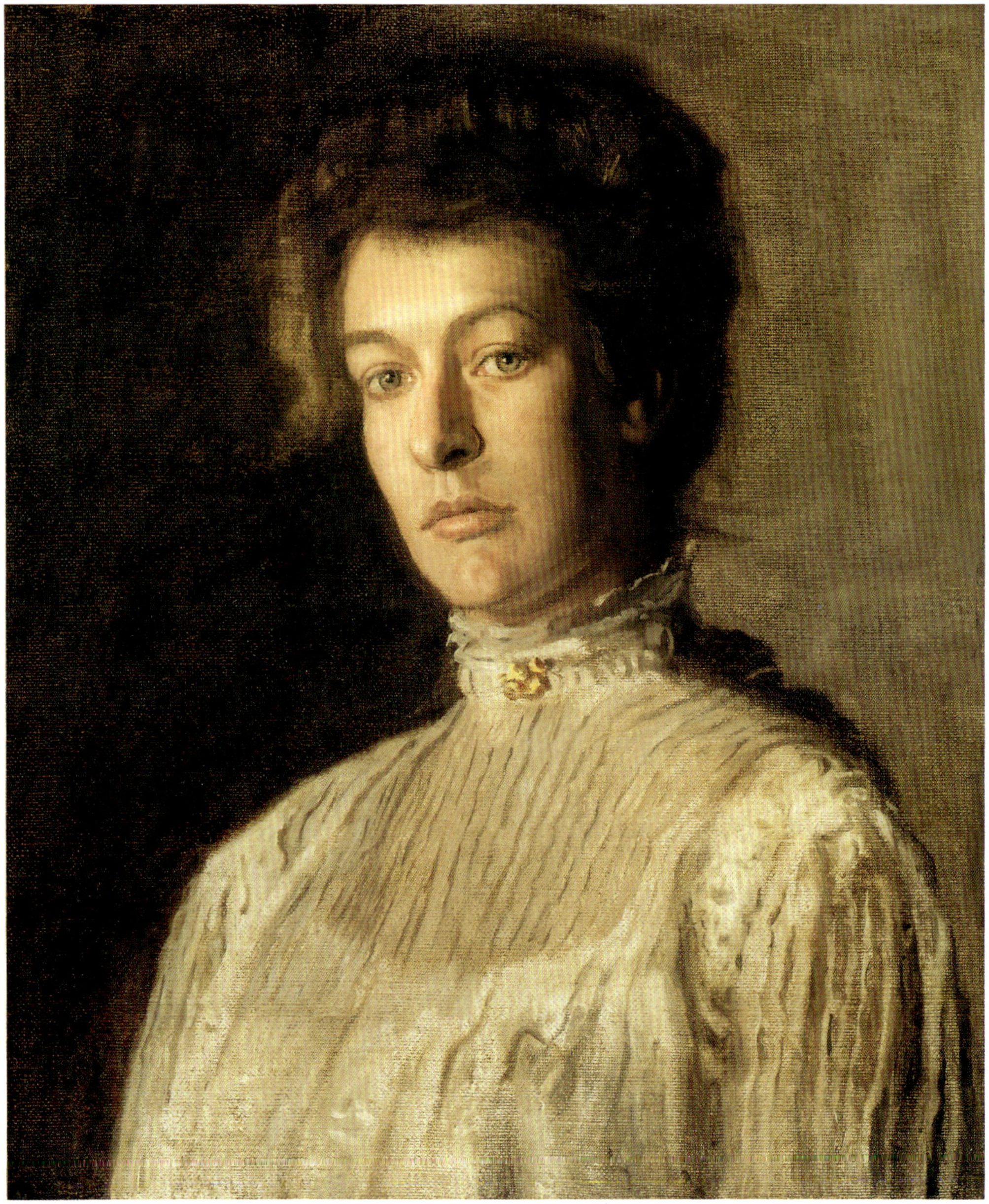

THOMAS EAKINS

(1844–1916)
Portrait of Mrs. Kern Dodge (Helen Peterson Greene), 1904
oil on canvas
24 x 20 in. (61 x 50.8 cm)
Dr. Herbert and Elizabeth Sussman

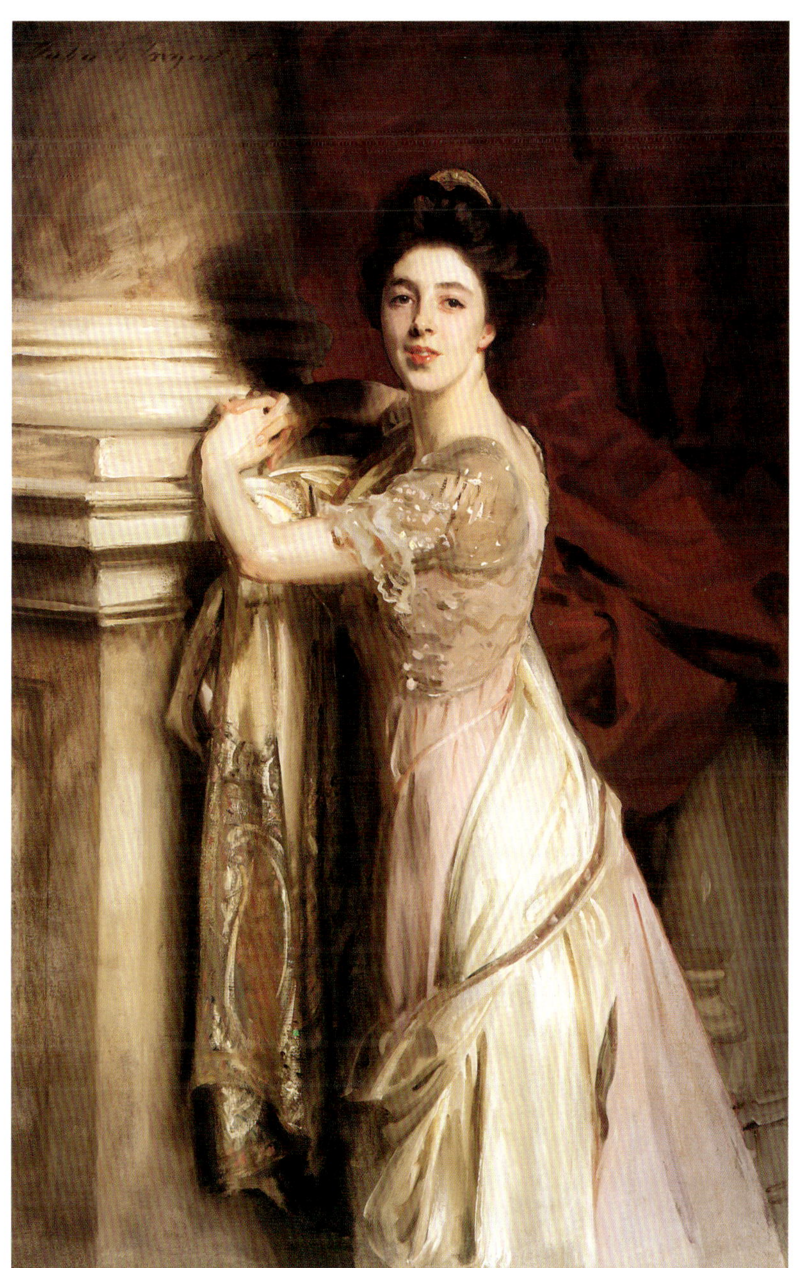

JOHN SINGER SARGENT

(1856–1925)
Portrait of Izme Vickers, 1907
oil on canvas
57½ x 37½ in. (146.1 x 95.3 cm)
Edna and Mickey Weiss

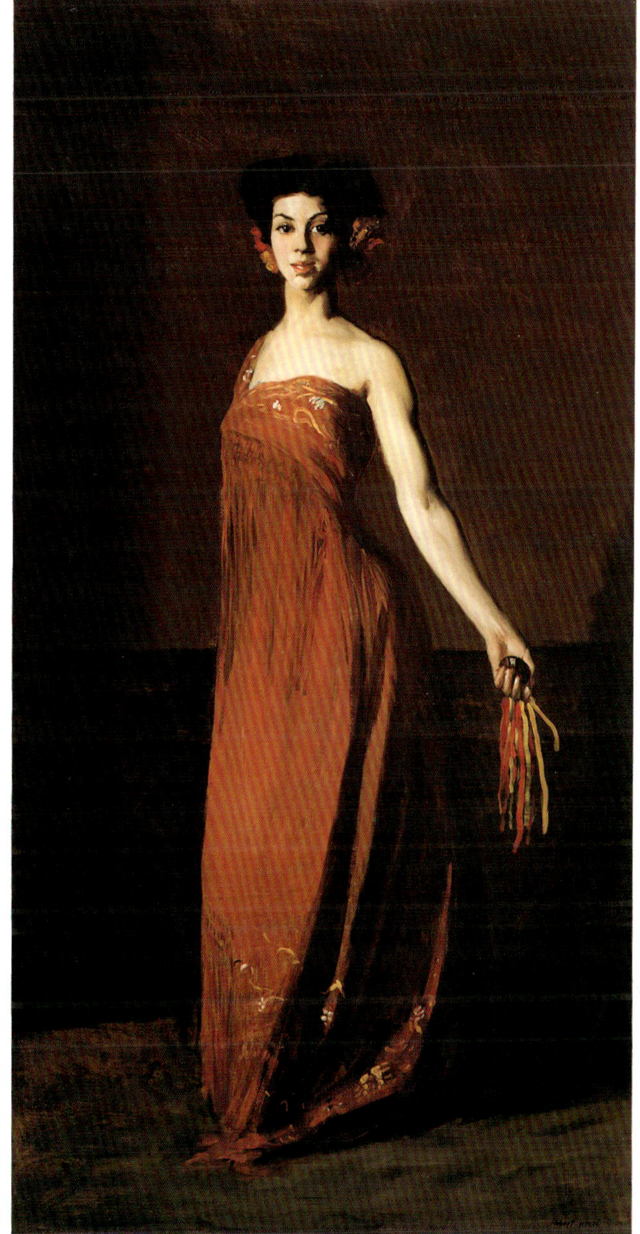

ROBERT HENRI

(1865–1929)
Spanish Dancer—Seviliana (Dancer with Castanet), 1904
oil on canvas
85 x 45 in. (215.9 x 114.3 cm)
Mr. and Mrs. Alan D. Levy

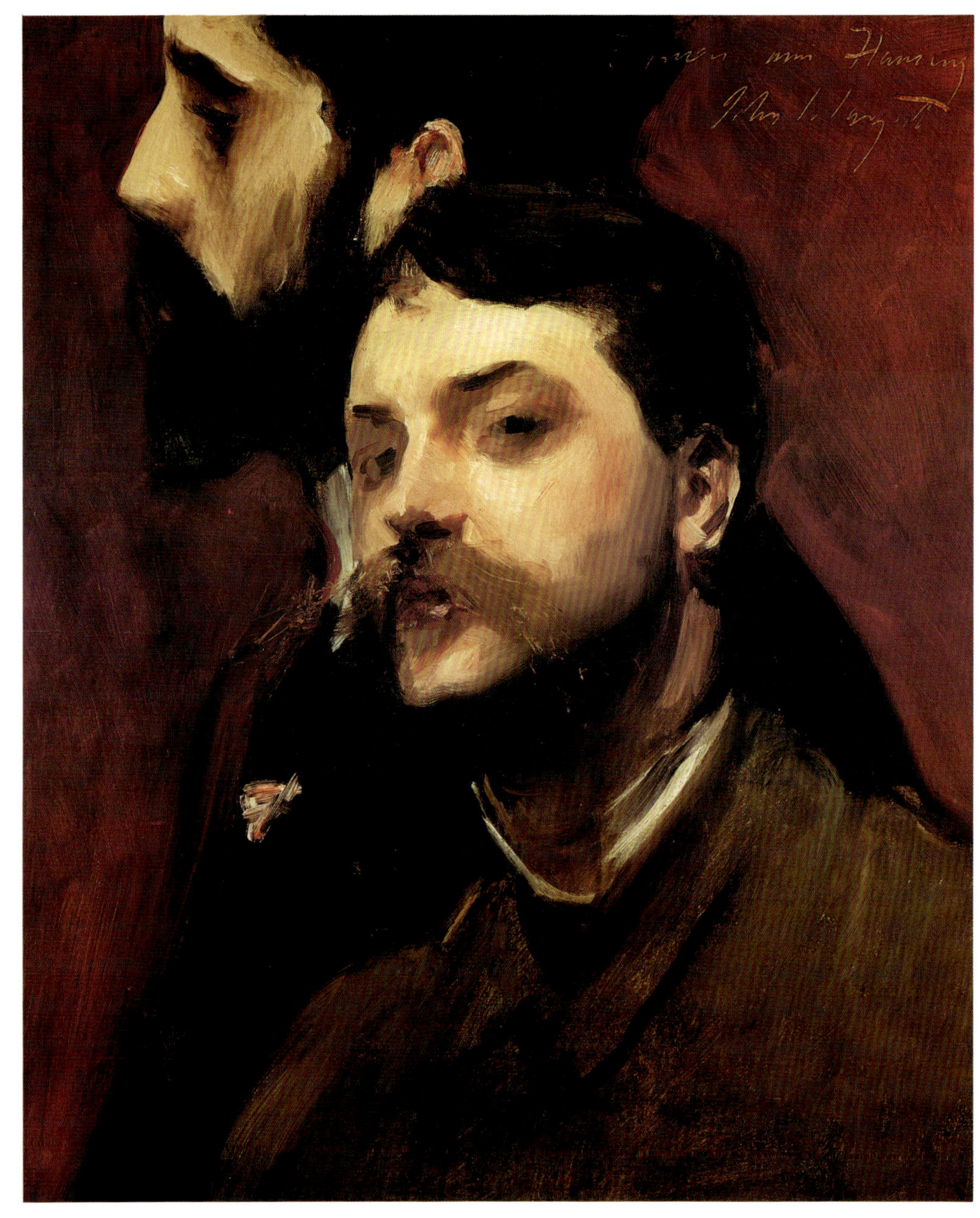

JOHN SINGER SARGENT

(1856–1925)
François Flameng and Paul Helleu, c. 1882–85
oil on canvas
21 x 17 in. (53.3 x 43.2 cm)
John and Gail Liebes

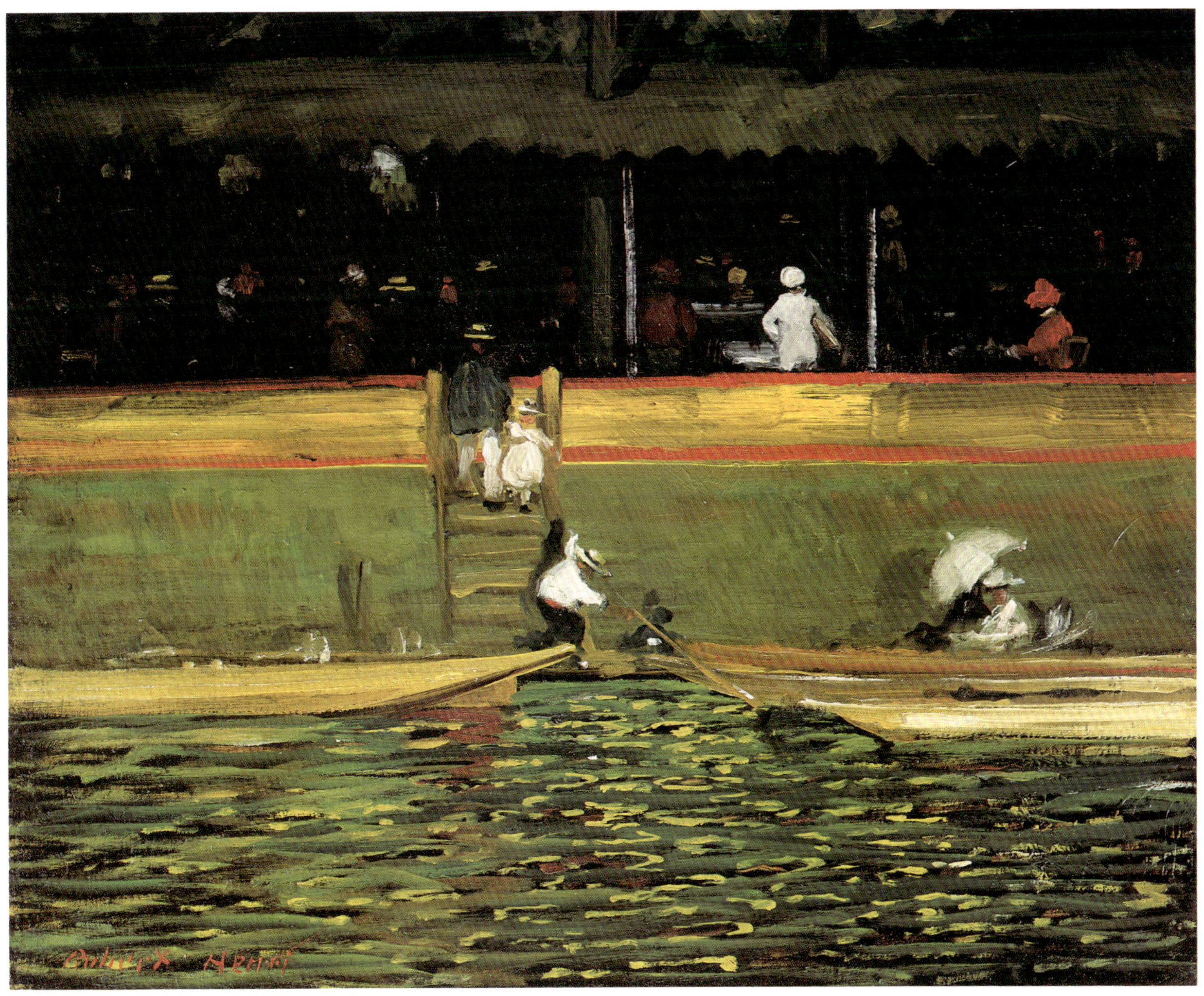

ROBERT HENRI

(1865–1929)
At Joinville, 1896
oil on canvas
26 x 31 in. (66 x 78.7 cm)
Ted and Carole Slavin

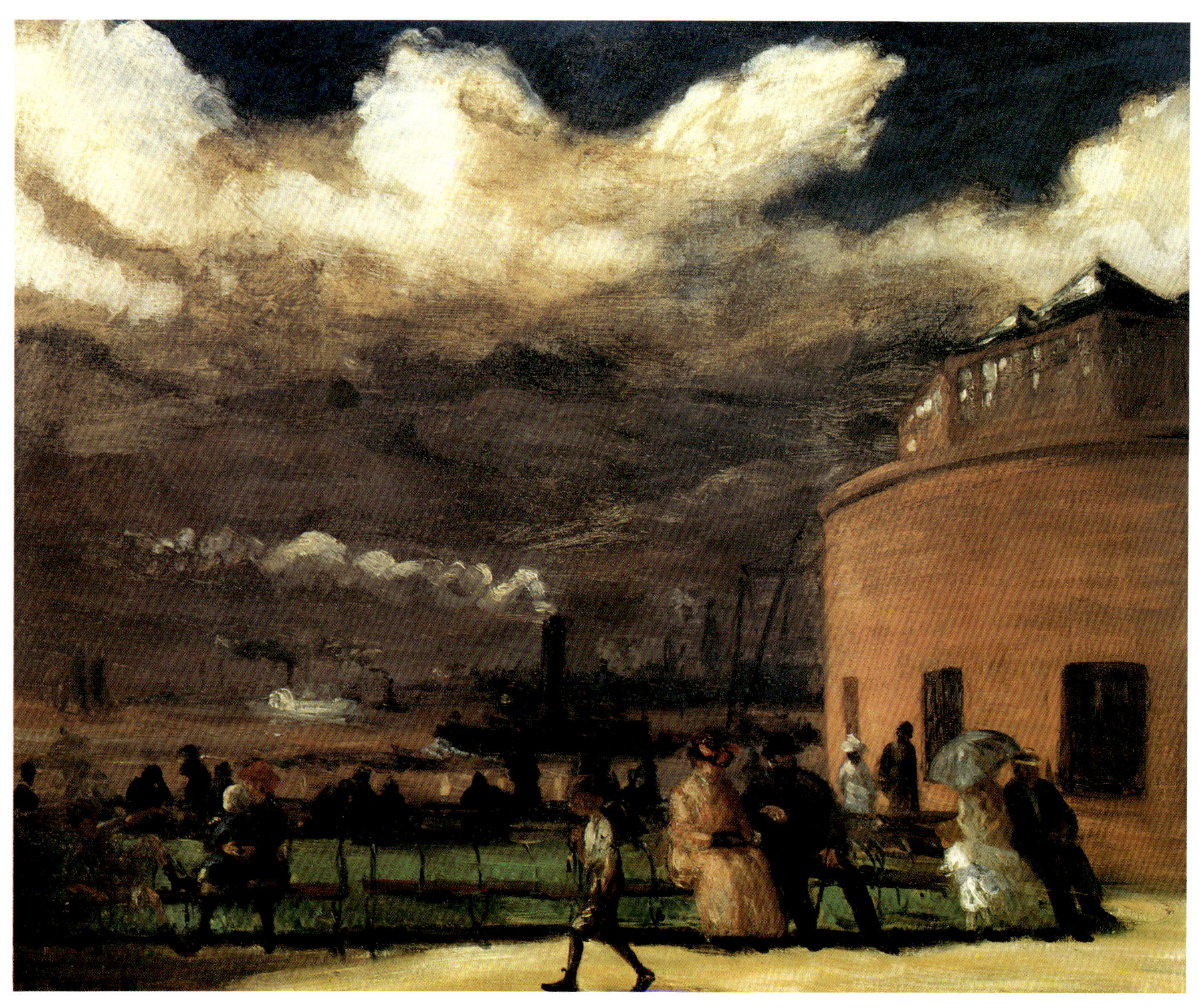

WILLIAM GLACKENS

(1870–1938)
Battery Park (The Battery), c. 1902–4
oil on canvas
26 x 32 in. (66 x 81.3 cm)
Mr. and Mrs. Alan D. Levy

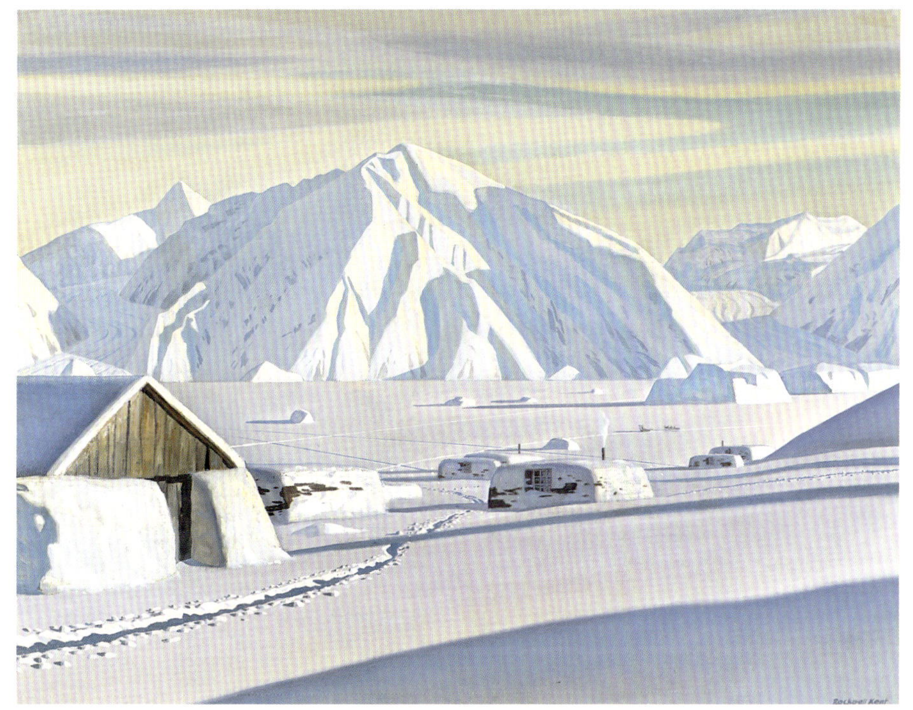

ROCKWELL KENT

(1882–1971)
Igdlorssuit, Winter, c. 1932–35
oil on canvas
34 x 44 in. (86.4 x 111.8 cm)
private collection

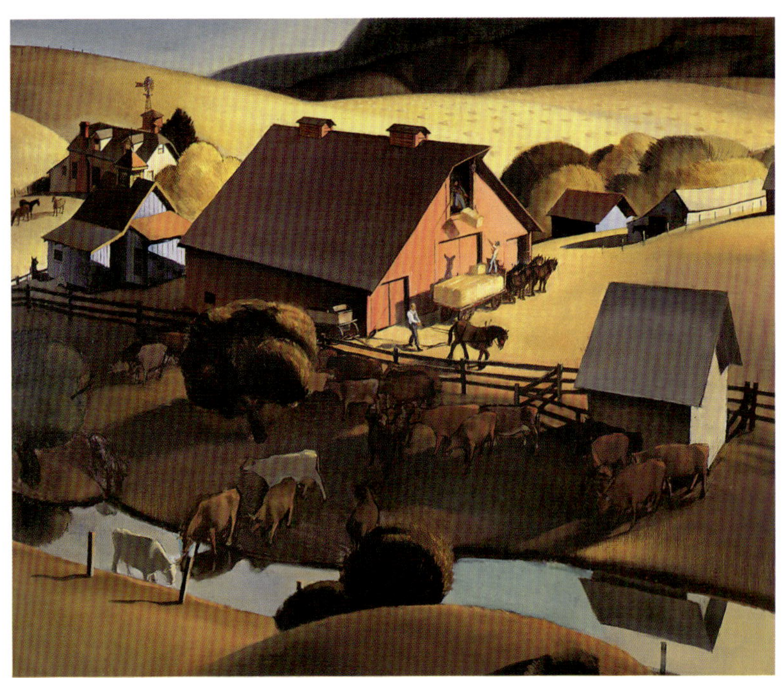

PHIL PARADISE

(b. 1905)
Ranch near San Luis Obispo, Evening Light, 1935
oil on canvas
28 x 34 in. (71.1 x 86.4 cm)
The Buck Collection

WILLIAM GROPPER

(1897–1977)
The Hunt, 1937
oil on Masonite
17½ x 36 in. (44.5 x 91.4 cm)
Bram and Sandra Dijkstra

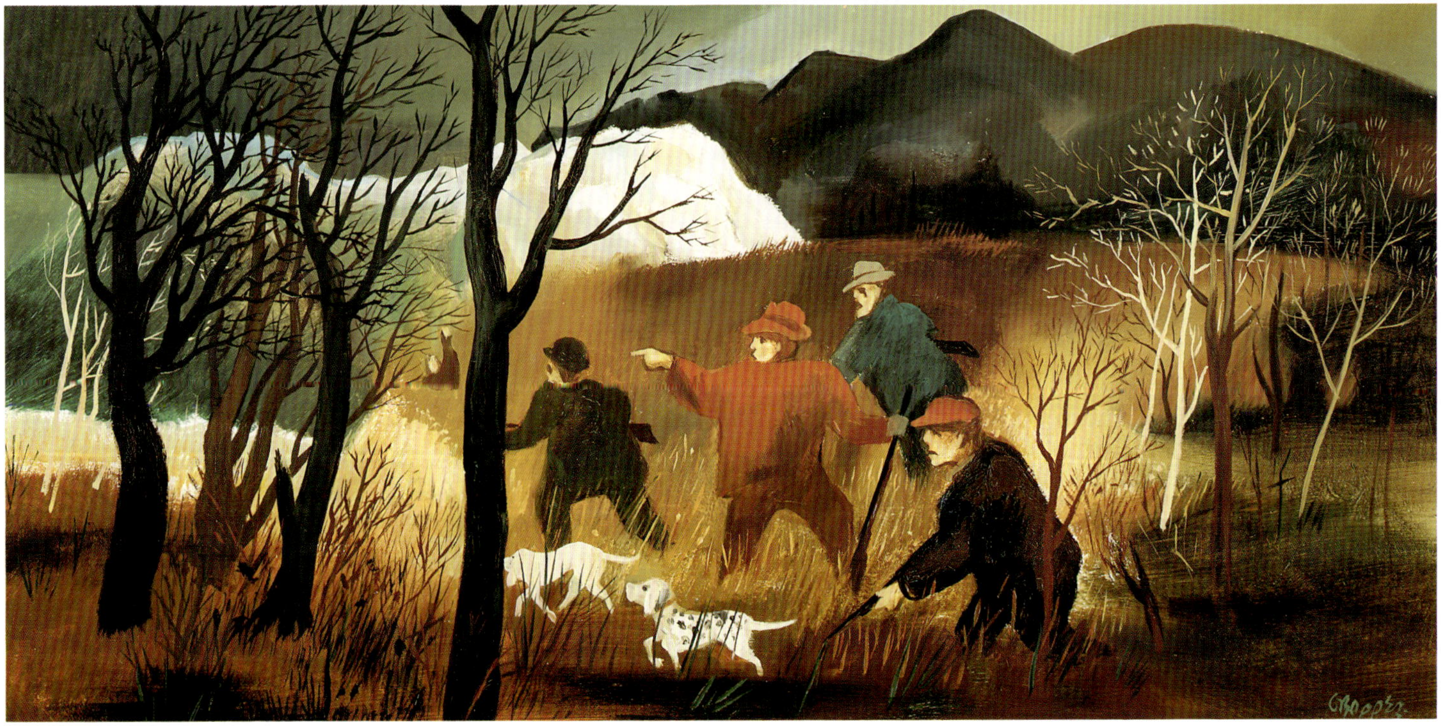

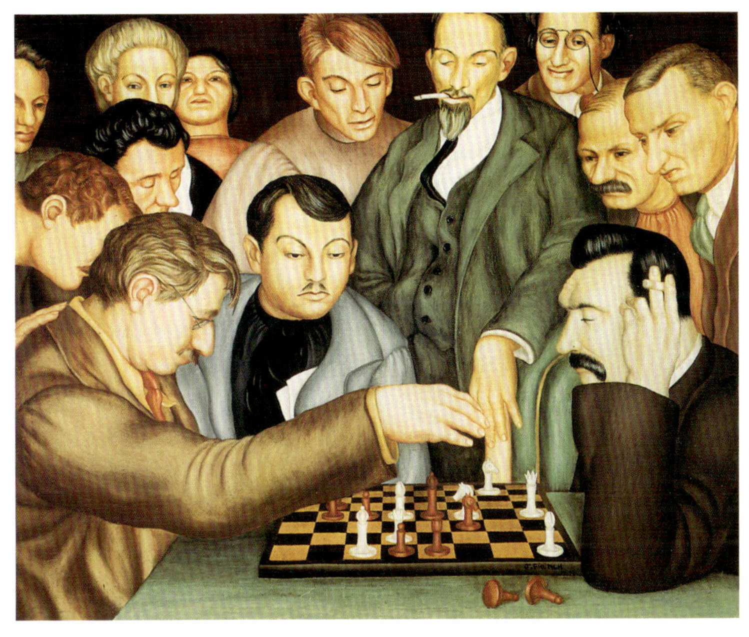

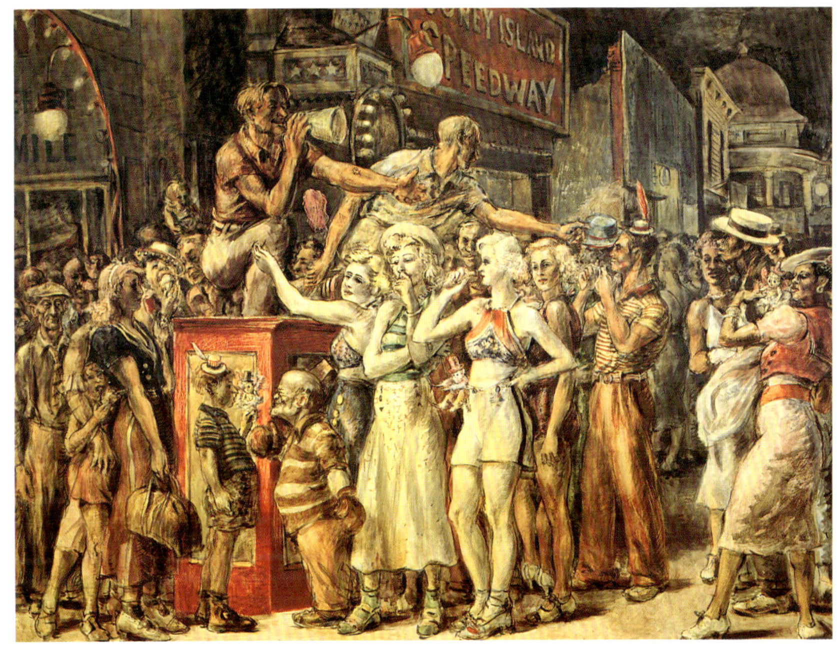

JARED FRENCH

(1905–1988)
Chess and Politics, c. 1933–39
oil on canvas
21⅞ x 26 in. (55.5 x 66.2 cm)
private collection,
courtesy Guggenheim, Asher Associates Inc.

REGINALD MARSH

(1898–1954)
Adults 10¢, Children 5¢, 1936
egg tempera on paper, mounted on Masonite
36 x 48 in. (91.4 x 121.9 cm)
Ted and Carole Slavin

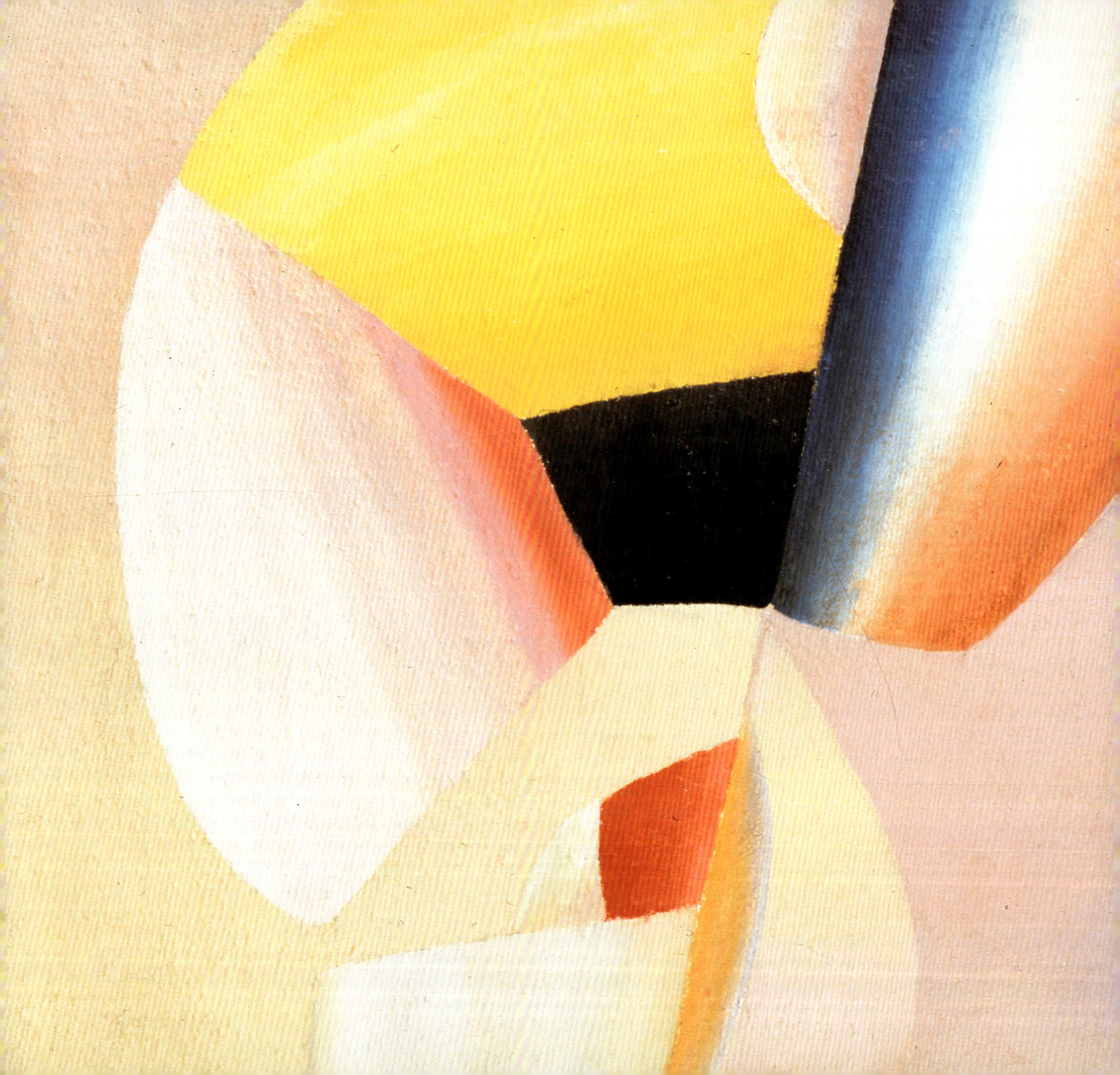

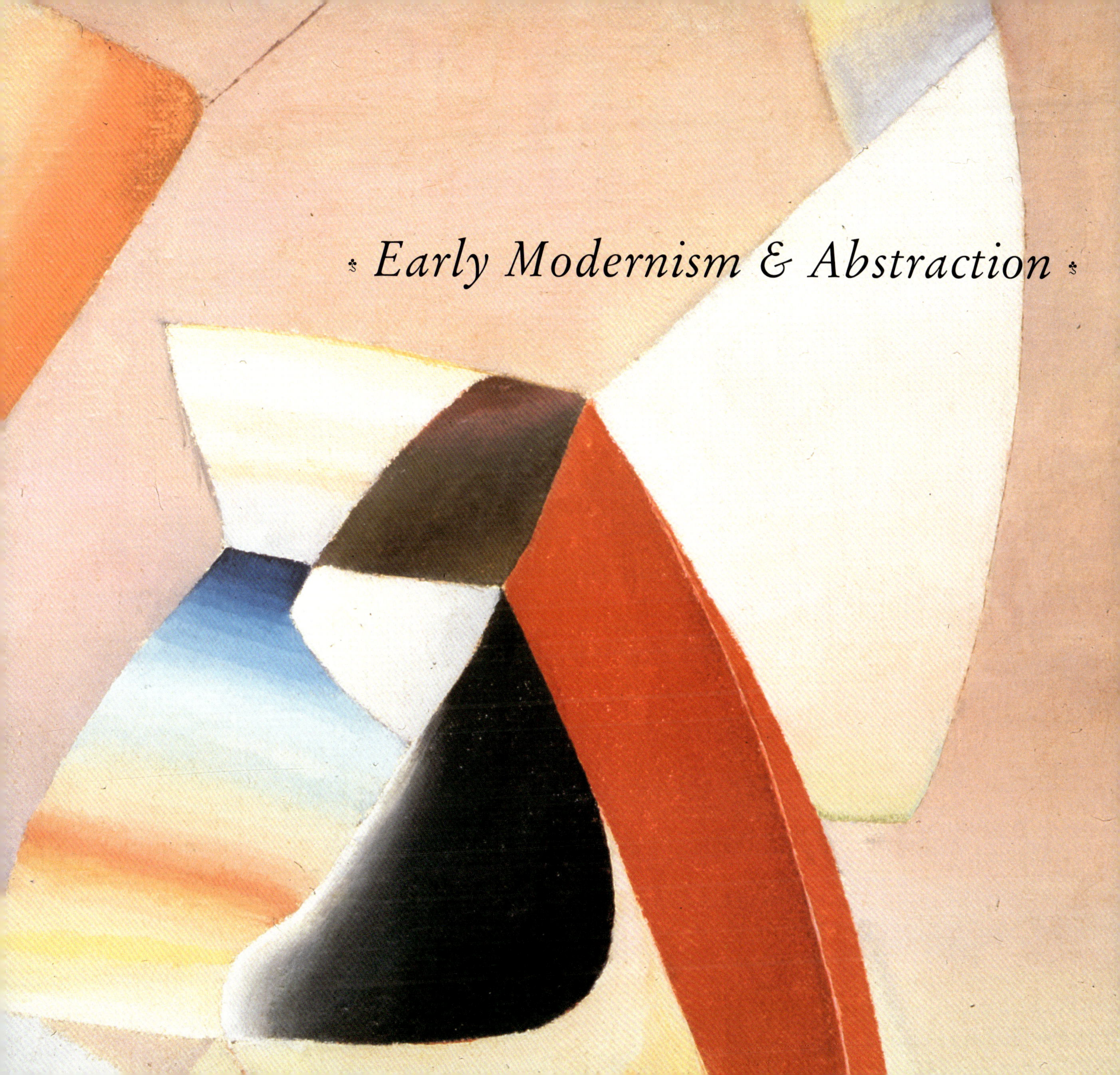
Early Modernism & Abstraction

In the decades preceding the First World War young American artists continued to flock to Europe, particularly Paris, to study. More than ever before they emulated the varied styles of the French avant-garde and other progressive European groups; they began to show a commitment to the idea that art in itself had a reality and importance independent of what it represented. Pushing the boundaries of the artistically acceptable, they replaced naturalistic rendering with colors revealing states of feeling and forms that were simplified, exaggerated, or otherwise distorted.

(previous pages)
JOHN FERREN
Abstraction, 1937
(detail)

The cubists fragmented their compositions to explore multiple views of their subjects, then juxtaposed these abstract planes in startling ways. Building on principles of color abstraction Stanton MacDonald-Wright and Morgan Russell, Americans working in Europe, aspired to create a universal art that explored the relationships between visual experience, emotion, and musical harmony. They investigated sculptural solidity and depth through color scales, always retaining a basis in the human figure. German expressionism intrigued Marsden Hartley, and he combined its strong use of color and brush with American themes, naive aesthetics, and a personal mystical sensibility.

After the 1913 Armory show in New York, American artists more freely developed their own idioms based on subjects and themes closer to home. The precisionists, working in the 1920s, often depicted skyscrapers, factories, and other structures typical of the new American industrial landscape. Preserving the integrity of the object but flattening and angularizing it, they eliminated perspective and surface detail. Georgia O'Keeffe, one of the best-known and popular American modernists, demonstrated this type of abstraction.

Surrealism challenged the viewer to find meaning in strange juxtapositions of seemingly unrelated objects; by the mid-1930s it had impacted American painting. The Californians Helen Lundeberg and her husband, Lorser Feitelson, were the only Americans to issue a surrealist manifesto, which proclaimed their "new classicism" to be based on subjective relationships and the functioning of the mind. In *Plant and Animal Analogies* (1934–35) Lundeberg created powerful feminine associations from organic forms and compared human development with that of the plant kingdom.

Other artists abandoned all references to the objective world. Credited as being the first completely nonobjective American artist, Manierre Dawson created *Prognostic* (1910) using nonreferential lines, shapes, and colors. But it was not until the 1930s that abstract art took hold in the United States. Its flowering during that period was due to the impact of constructivism and neoplasticism, in particular the art of Piet Mondrian.

After World War II American artists, having absorbed the lessons of the Europeans, took the lead in modernist art-making, signaling the permanent importance of American painting in the international art world. ❦ –T.A.

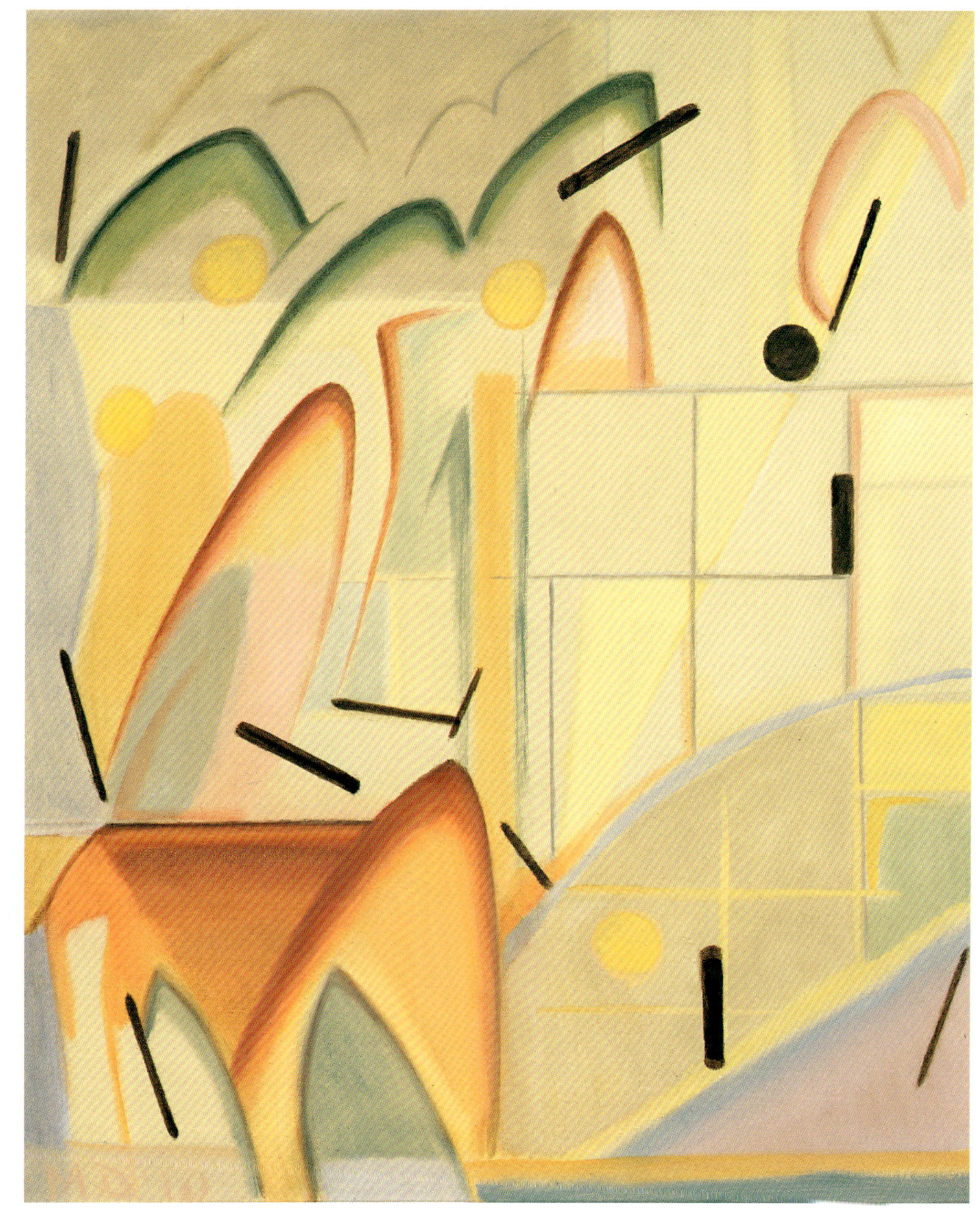

MANIERRE DAWSON

(1887–1969)
Prognostic [left panel of triptych], 1910
oil on canvas
24 x 20 in. (61 x 50.8 cm)
Dr. Peter B. Fischer

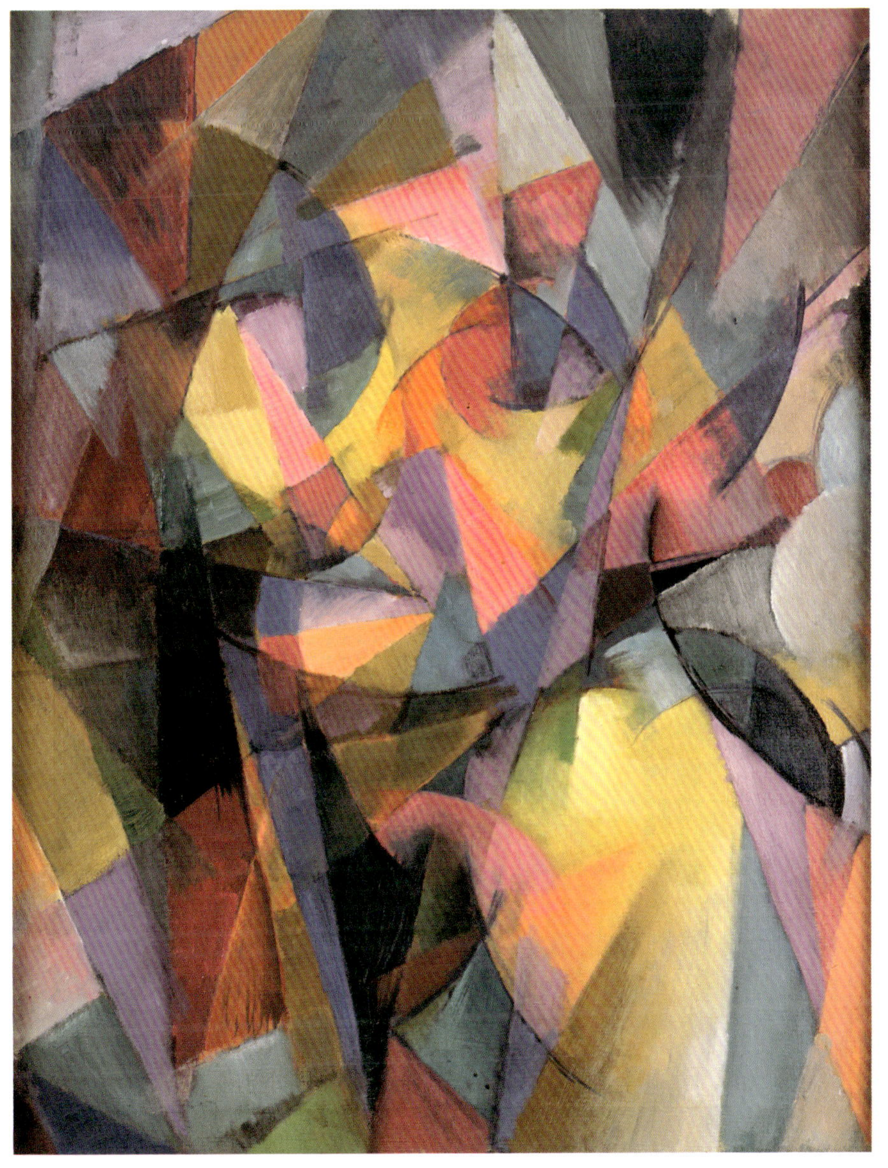

STANTON MACDONALD-WRIGHT

(1890–1973)
Synchromy (possibly *Portrait of Artist*), c. 1919
oil on canvas
36 x 28 in. (91.4 x 71.1 cm)
private collection

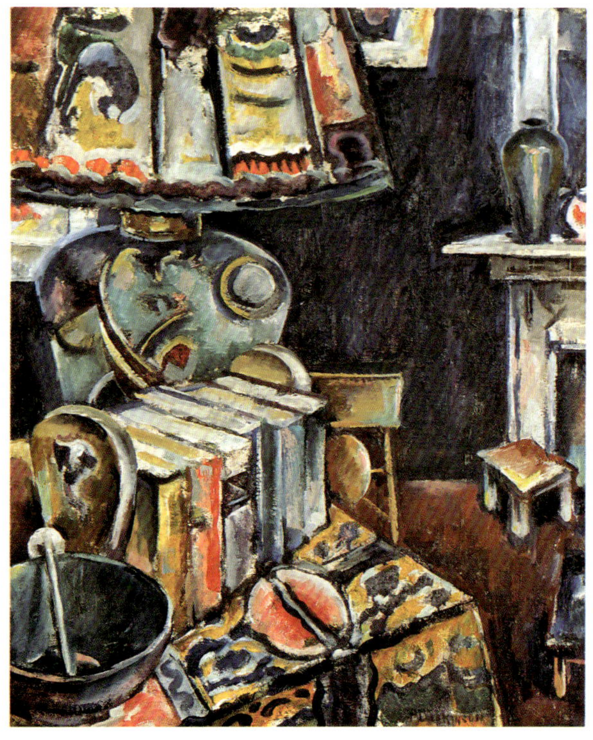

PRESTON DICKINSON

(1891–1930)
Interior, c. 1919
oil on canvas
24 x 20 in. (61 x 50.8 cm)
Margery and Maurice Katz

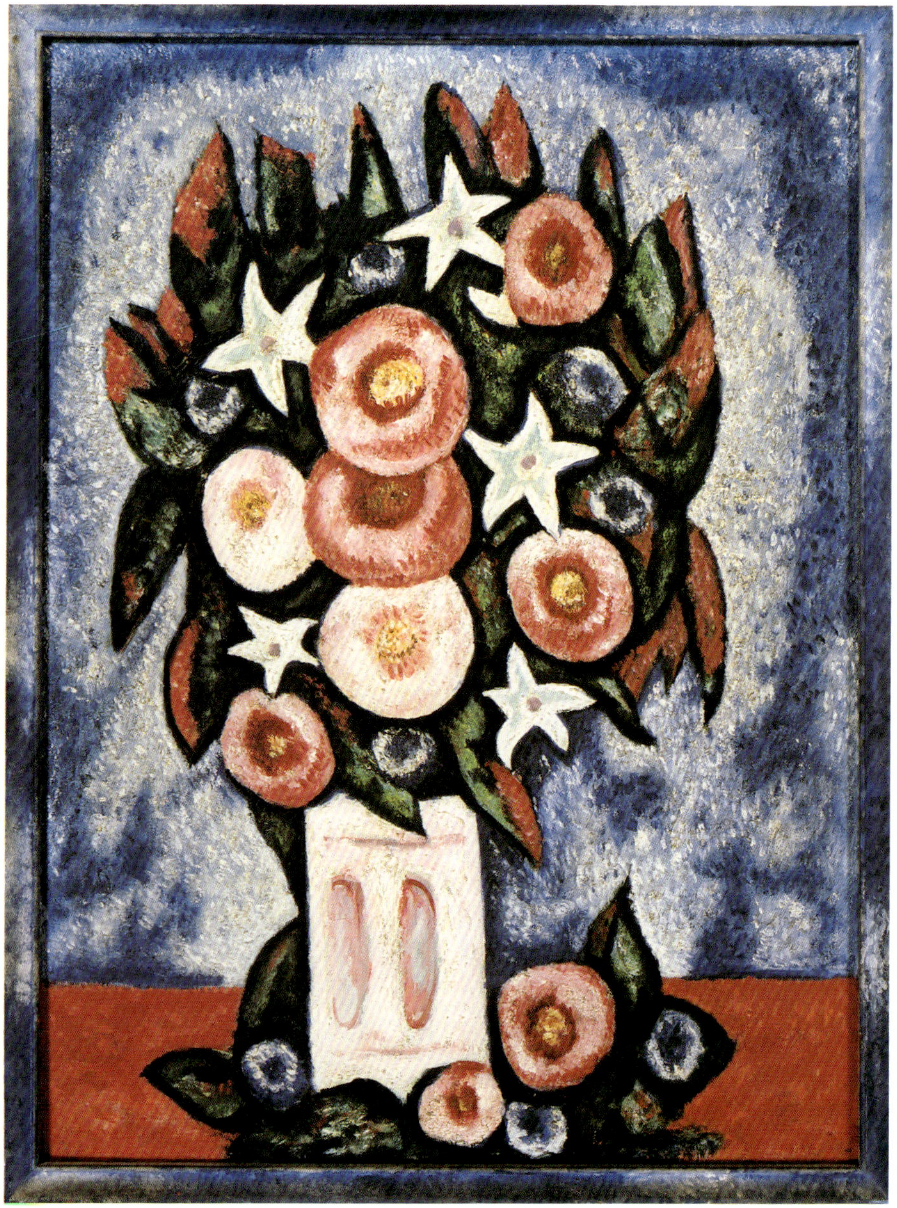

MARSDEN HARTLEY

(1877–1943)
Night and Some Flowers, c. 1940
oil on canvasboard
25¼ x 19⅜ in. (64.1 x 49.2 cm) with painted frame
private collection

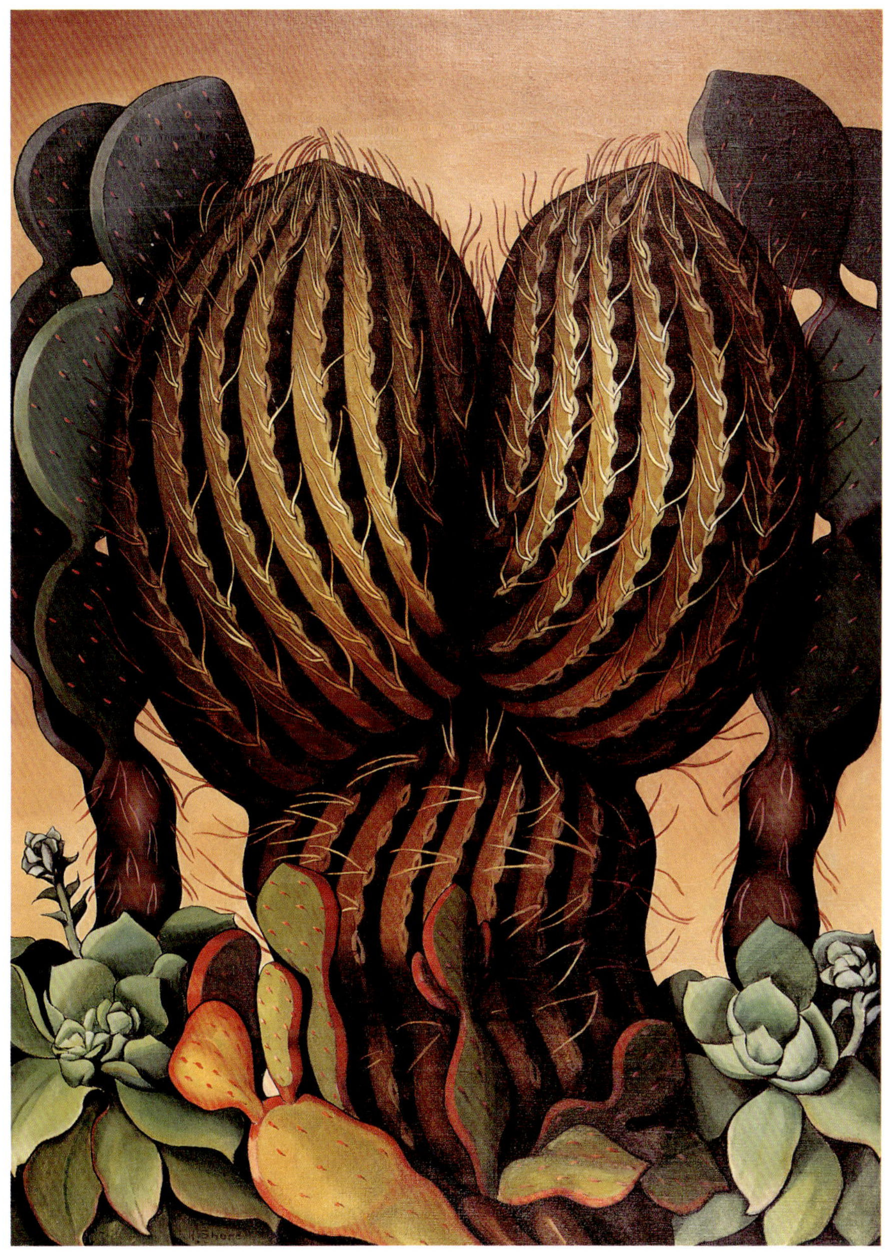

HENRIETTA SHORE

(1880–1963)
Cactus, 1926
oil on canvas
38 x 28 in. (96.5 x 71.1 cm)
private collection

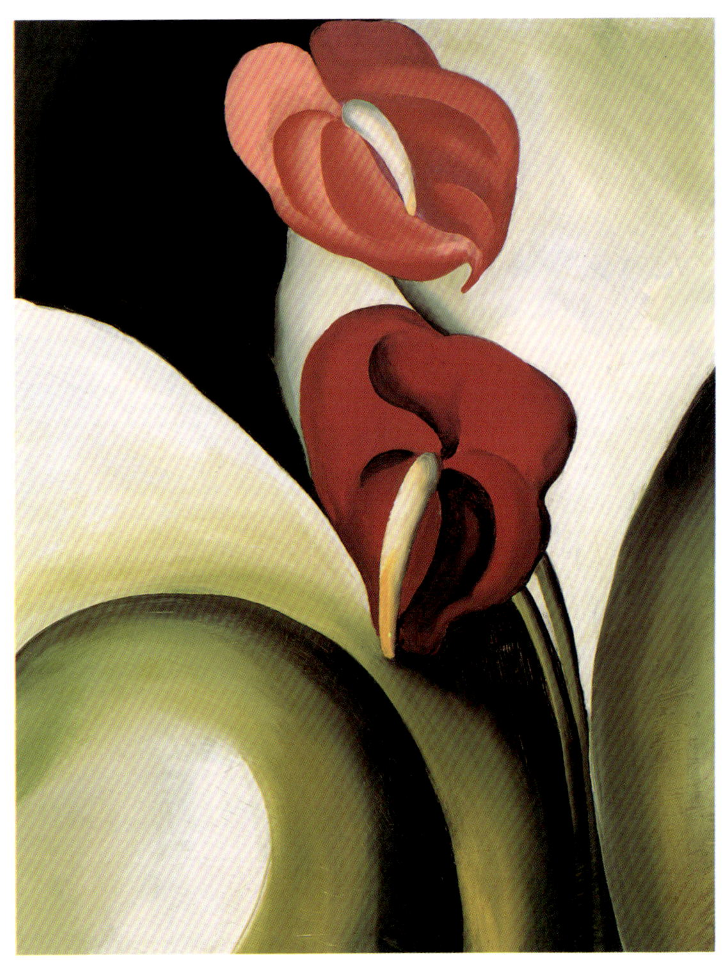

GEORGIA O'KEEFFE

(1887–1986)
Antherium, 1924
oil on canvas
20½ x 16½ in. (52.1 x 41.9 cm)
Leona Palmer

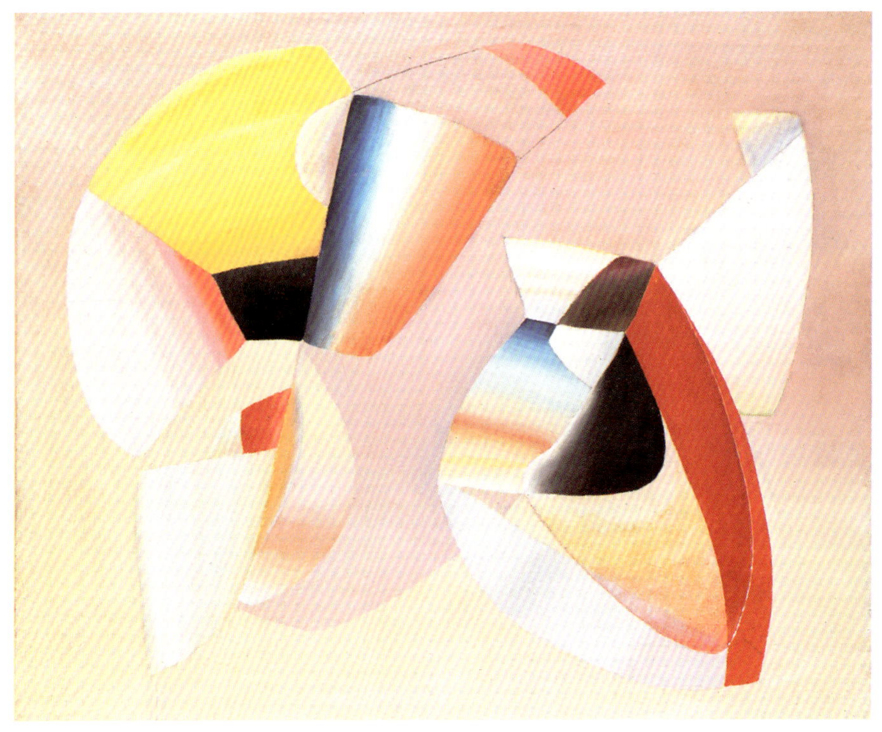

JOHN FERREN

(1905–1970)
Abstraction, 1937
oil on canvas
22 x 26 in. (55.9 x 66 cm)
Dr. Peter B. Fischer

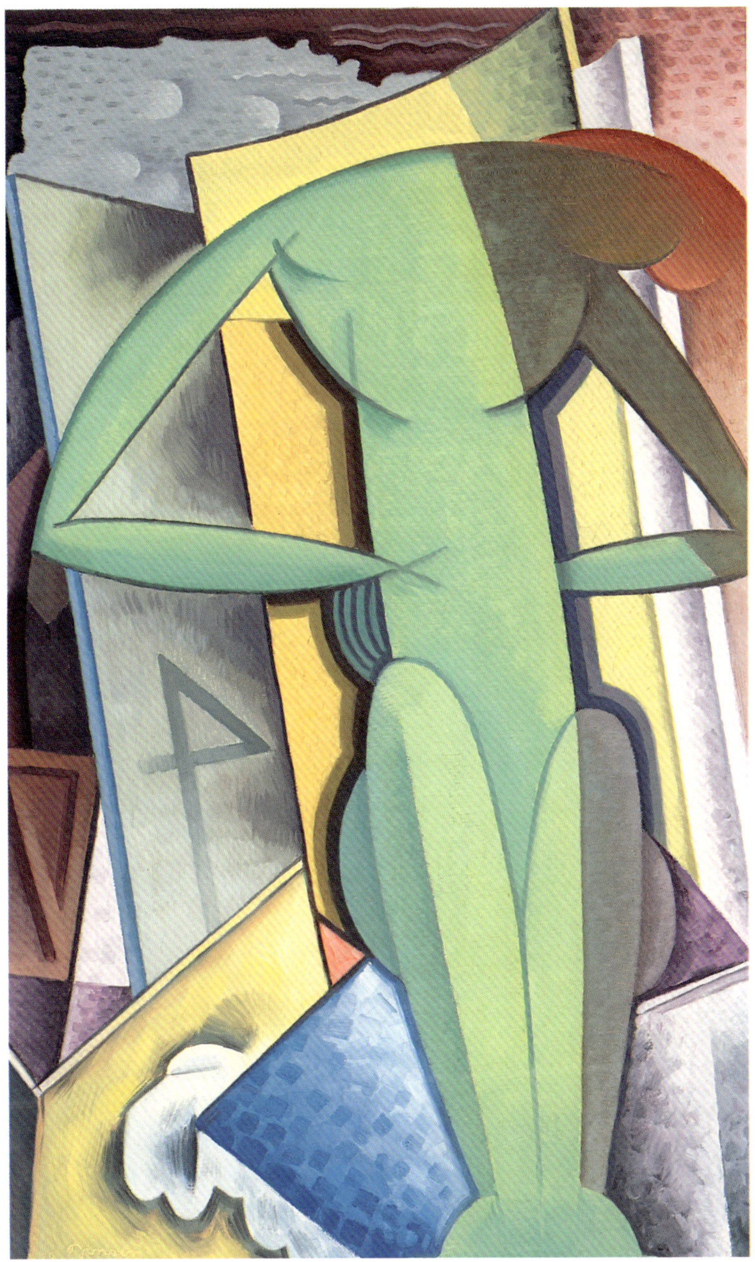

RAYMOND JONSON

(1891–1982)
Abstraction, No. 4, 1929
oil on canvas
24 x 15 in. (61 x 38.1 cm)
lent anonymously

HARRY HOLTZMAN

(1912–1987)
Square Volume with Yellow and Blue, 1938–40
oil and acrylic on Masonite
$23\frac{7}{8}$ x $23\frac{7}{8}$ in. (60.6 x 60.6 cm)
Dr. Peter B. Fischer

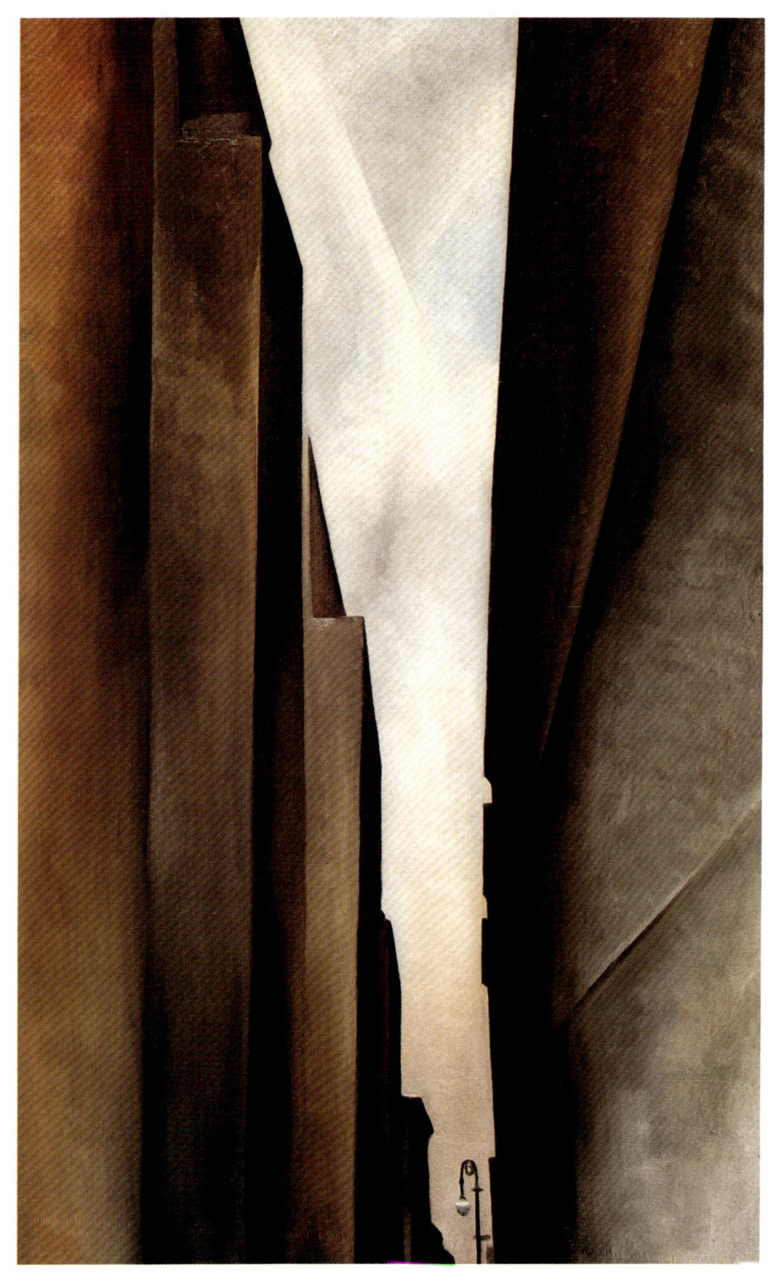

GEORGIA O'KEEFFE

(1887–1986)
Street, New York, No. 1, 1926
oil on canvas
48⅛ x 29⅞ in. (122.2 x 75.9 cm)
private collection

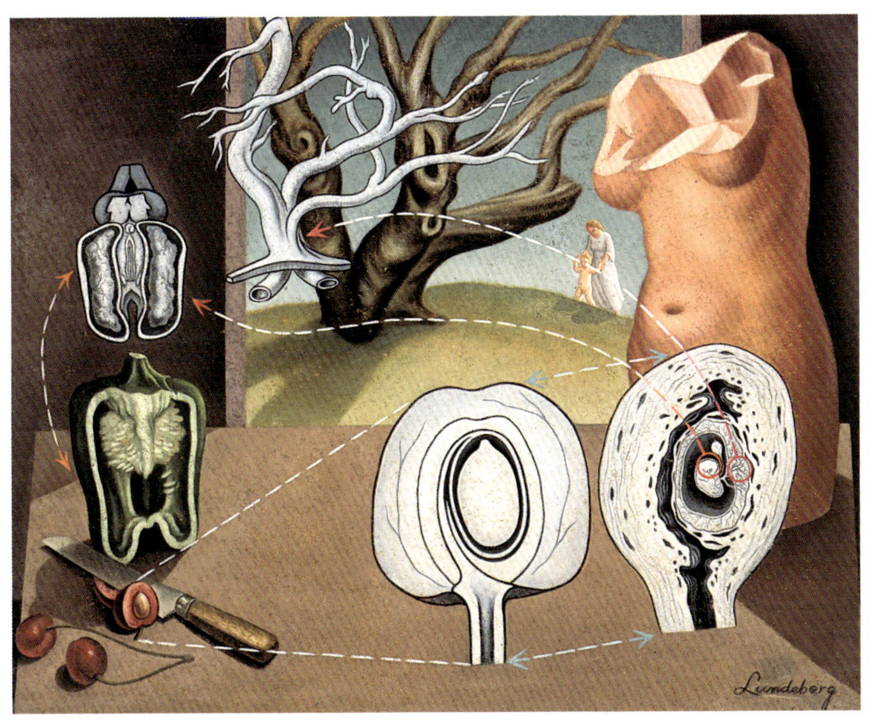

HELEN LUNDEBERG

(b. 1908)
Plant and Animal Analogies, 1934–35
oil on Celotex
24 x 30 in. (61 x 76.2 cm)
The Buck Collection

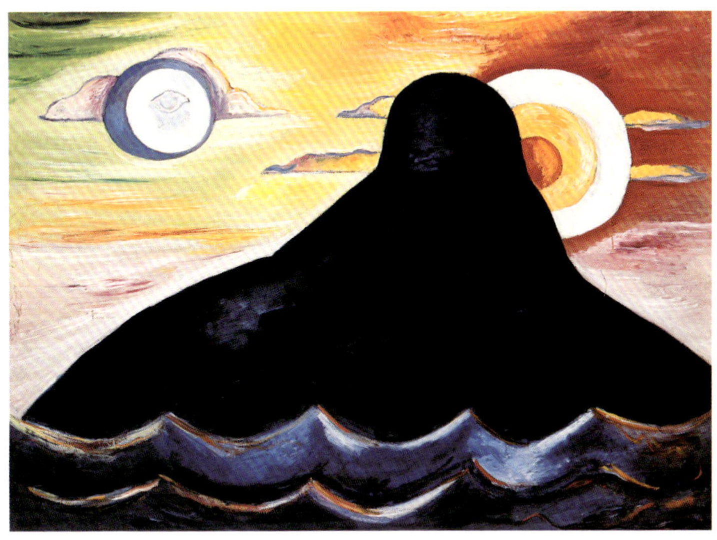

MARSDEN HARTLEY

(1877–1943)
The Mountain of the North
(After Design of Cosmas the Monk, 900 A.D.*)*, 1932
oil on cardboard
24½ x 33½ in. (62.2 x 85.1 cm)
private collection

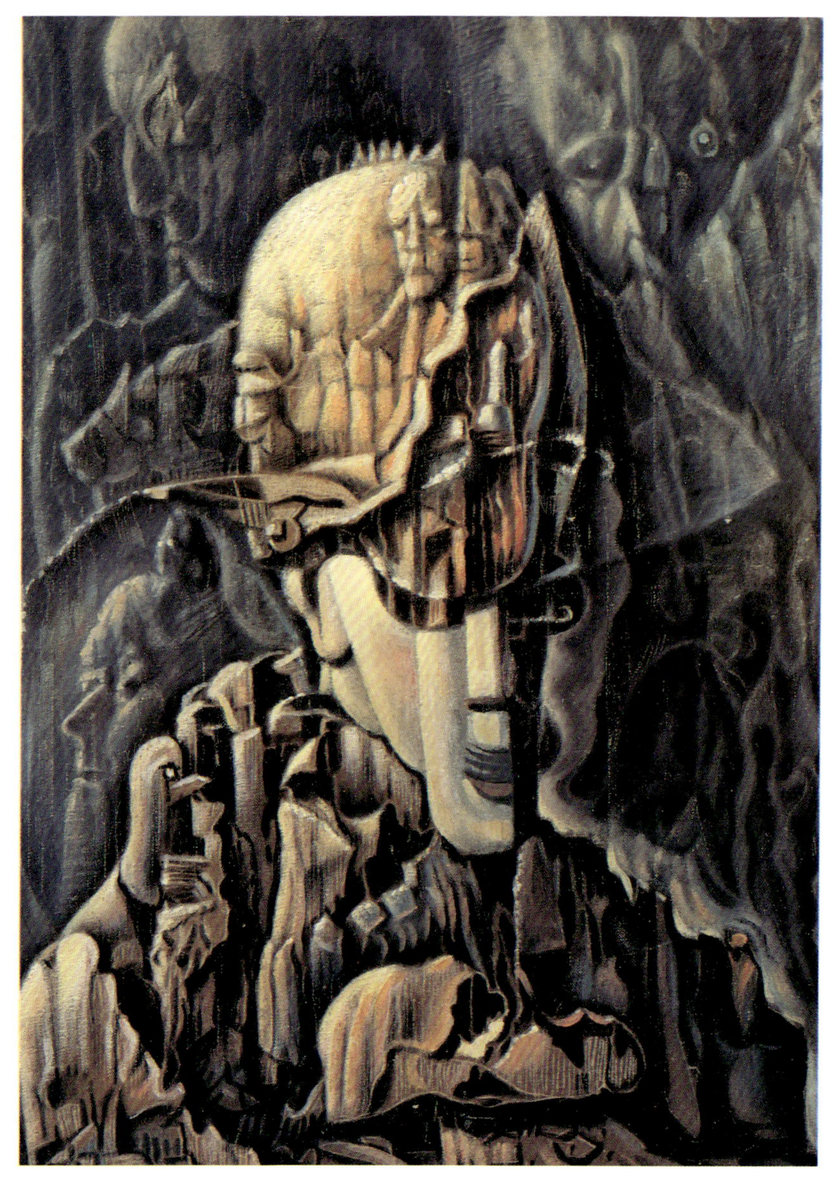

BEN BERLIN

(1887–1939)
Surreal Portrait, 1938
oil on canvasboard
19½ x 14½ in. (49.5 x 36.8 cm)
Fannie and Alan Leslie,
promised gift to the
Los Angeles County Museum of Art

Acknowledgments

An exhibition devoted to local collections is a special type of event, offering a museum the unique opportunity of celebrating regional taste. I would like to thank the American Art Council for suggesting that the time was appropriate for reexamining collecting trends in Southern California, and the board of trustees for agreeing with them. Under the leadership of William A. Mingst, president, the board has been helpful. Stephanie Barron, coordinator of curatorial affairs, was also supportive and provided thoughtful suggestions throughout the planning period.

The exhibition and catalogue were made possible through the generosity of many. I would like to thank the Willametta K. Day Foundation and Cecile Bartman for underwriting the exhibition. I am also especially grateful to Abby and Alan D. Levy, Carole and Ted Slavin, and Bente and Gerald E. Buck for supporting the publication of this catalogue.

American Paintings in Southern California Collections: From Gilbert Stuart to Georgia O'Keeffe could not have been realized without the cooperation of many dedicated private collectors. I would like to thank the lenders to this exhibition for parting with their paintings for three months so that others could enjoy them. In many instances the sacrifice was deeply felt, as when I asked for a collector's favorite work or for the one that hung over the living-room fireplace.

I also appreciate the response of the many enthusiastic collectors whose paintings do not appear in the present exhibition. They kindly welcomed us into their homes and answered our many questions. I thank them for their hospitality and regret that numerous wonderful works had to be omitted because of space limitations.

Our original intent was not only to exhibit some of the best American paintings in private hands but also to bring to the public's attention little-known gems. Thus during the preparation of this exhibition I sought out collectors new to me. In this search I was assisted by many people. An informal advisory committee was organized that included my colleagues Whitney Ganz of William Karges Fine Arts; Barbara Guggenheim of Guggenheim, Asher Associates Inc.; Martin Peterson, curator of American art at the San Diego Museum of Art; and Patricia Trenton, curator of the art collection of the Los Angeles Athletic Club. They were quite generous in sharing their knowledge of collectors in the area and assisting me with introductions and loans. For this I owe a hearty thanks to each of them. In addition I would like to thank Robert Hennings, chief curator of the Santa Barbara Museum, and Nancy Moure and Michael Quick, former curators of American Art at the Los Angeles County Museum of Art, for their suggestions. Many collectors also provided me with introductions, and special thanks go to Virginia Carpenter, LACMA trustee, who was particularly helpful. My fellow curators Stephanie Barron and Carol Eliel, in twentieth-century art, and Mary Levkoff and Patrice Marandel, in European painting and sculpture, were also generous in sharing contacts.

There were many others at LACMA who assisted in the organization and presentation of the exhibition and the publication of this catalogue. Thanks must go to Sheri Bernstein and Trudi Abram, who assisted in researching the collections and organizing the exhibition; Ms. Abram contributed the thoughtful introductions to the thematic sections of the catalogue. I also appreciate the conscientiousness and devotion of department secretaries Linda Rapagna and Cheryl Stone, who made all the administrative details flow so easily. Thanks also to painting conservators Joseph Fronek, Virginia

Rasmussen, and Shelley Svoboda, who carefully examined and in some cases conserved the paintings for the exhibition. Registrar Renee Montgomery and assistant registrar Sandy Davis handled the logistics of transportation, while Leslie Bowman and Beverley Sabo of the exhibitions department assisted in the early planning stages. As always, Bernard Kester provided us with a sensitive and truly beautiful installation design, and Arthur Owens, assistant director/operations, and his staff skillfully mounted the exhibition. Anne Diederick was very helpful in handling our library requests. The catalogue was thoughtfully edited by Thomas Frick and handsomely designed by Amy McFarland, with expert photography contributed by Jay McNally.

A substantial part of my essay on the history of collecting American art in Southern California deals with material not well documented, so in many cases I had to depend on the memories of the actual participants in that history. Again the collectors, especially Jo Ann and Julian Ganz Jr., were most important. Scott M. Levitt of Butterfield and Butterfield and Harvey Jones of the Oakland Museum were among the many who provided me with crucial facts. Finally, I would also like to thank Larry Curry, founding curator of American art at LACMA, Michael Quick, curator from 1976 to 1993, and John Wilmerding, professor of art history at Princeton University, for reading drafts.

Ilene Susan Fort

Lenders to the exhibition

Patricia & Richard Anawalt
Sidney & Diana Avery Trust
Mrs. Cecile C. Bartman
Dr. & Mrs. Edward H. Boseker
Mr. & Mrs. Gerald E. Buck
Mr. & Mrs. Hal Burroughs
Iris & B. Gerald Cantor
Mr. & Mrs. William M. Carpenter
Dr. & Mrs. Robert M. Carroll
Mrs. Edward W. Carter
Mr. & Mrs. Willard Clark
Mr. & Mrs. Theodore G. Congdon
Nancy Daly
Bram & Sandra Dijkstra
Dr. Peter B. Fischer
Camilla Chandler Frost
Jo Ann & Julian Ganz Jr.
Mrs. Joan Irvine Smith
Judith & Steaven Jones
Margery & Maurice Katz
Mr. & Mrs. Arnold C. Kirkeby
Fannie & Alan Leslie
Mr. & Mrs. Alan D. Levy
Mr. & Mrs. John M. Liebes
Mr. & Mrs. William Dana Lippman
Nancy & Arthur Manella
Mrs. Thomas J. McEwan
Dr. & Mrs. M. S. Mickiewicz
Joseph L. Moure
Mrs. Barbara Pauley Pagen
Leona Palmer
Mr. & Mrs. J. Douglas Pardee
Mr. & Mrs. Stewart Resnick
James & Linda Ries
Samuel & Elaine Rosenthal Trust
Brenda & Gary Ruttenberg
Jean & Samuel Sapin
Ted & Carol Slavin
Bernard Solomon
Mr. Craig A. Starkey
Dr. Herbert & Elizabeth Sussman
Mr. & Mrs. Robert Bruce Tebbe
Elisabeth Waldo-Dentzel
Christopher & Gretchen Ward
Edna and Mickey Weiss
Bobbi & Walter Zifkin

bequest of Charles C. & Elma Ralphs Shoemaker

and various anonymous lenders

❦ *Promised Gifts* ❦

Mr. & Mrs. William M. Carpenter

Edward Moran (1829–1901)
**View of Windsor Castle,* 1863
oil on canvas
41 x 68½ in. (104.1 x 174 cm)

Jo Ann & Julian Ganz Jr.

Fitz Hugh Lane (1804–1865)
**Boston Harbor, Sunset,* 1850–55
oil on canvas
24 x 39¼ in. (61 x 99.7 cm)

Fannie & Alan Leslie

Ben Berlin (1887–1939)
Surreal Portrait, 1938
oil on canvasboard
19½ x 14½ in. (49.5 x 36.8 cm)

Charles Howard (1889–1978)
Double Circle, 1950
oil on canvas
24 x 34 in. (61 x 86.4 cm)

Charles Howard
Untitled, 1931
gouache and watercolor on paper
14 x 20 in. (35.6 x 50.8 cm)

Will Henry Stevens (1881–1949)
Marine Abstraction, 1944
oil on board
27 x 21 in. (68.6 x 53.3 cm)

Will Henry Stevens
Undersea, 1945
tempera and gouache on paper laid down on board
27¼ x 21 in. (69.2 x 53.3 cm)

Charles White (1918–1979)
Lovers, 1942
egg tempera on board
19¾ x 26 in. (50.2 x 66 cm)

Nancy Dustin Wall Moure

Maurice Braun (1877–1941)
Untitled (Landscape), c. 1925
oil on canvas
40 x 50 in. (101.6 x 127 cm)

James & Linda Ries

Edgar Alwyn Payne (1882–1947)
The Great White Peak, No. 2, 1924
oil on canvas
62 x 62 in. (157.5 x 157.5 cm)

Lillian Apodaca Weiner

Stanton MacDonald-Wright (1890–1973)
**Still Life with Fruit,* 1923
oil on canvas
16 x 22 in. (40.6 x 55.9 cm)

**Twenty-fifth Anniversary Promised Gift*

Selected Bibliography

Catalogues devoted to specific collections are listed under the collector's name.

ADAMS. Baird, Joseph Armstrong, Jr., comp. *The West Remembered: Artists and Images, 1837–1973; Selections from the Collection of Earl C. Adams.* Exh. cat. San Francisco: California Historical Society, 1973.

BLOCH. Bloch, E. Maurice. *Faces and Figures in American Drawings.* Exh. cat. San Marino: Huntington Library and Art Gallery, 1989.

DENTZEL. *The Lure of the West: The Carl S. Dentzel Collection of Western American Art.* Exh. cat. Phoenix and Pasadena: Phoenix Art Museum and Southwest Museum, Pasadena, 1987.

EVERETT. Peterson, Martin. "The Everett Collection." *Art of California* 3 (May 1990): 48–55.

FACTOR. See Santa Barbara Museum of Art 1967.

FISCHER. *Progressive Geometric Abstraction in America, 1934–1955: Selections from the Peter B. Fischer Collection.* Exh. cat. Clinton, New York: Fred L. Emerson Gallery, Hamilton College, 1987. Essays by Harry Holtzman and Susan C. Larsen. Interview with the collector by Necia Gelker.

Fort, Ilene Susan, and Michael Quick. *American Art: A Catalogue of the Los Angeles County Museum of Art.* Los Angeles: Los Angeles County Museum of Art, 1991.

GANZ. *Chosen Works of American Art, 1850–1924, from the Collection of Jo Ann and Julian Ganz Jr.* Exh. cat. Los Angeles: Los Angeles County Museum of Art, 1969. Introduction by Larry Curry.

———. *American Paintings, Watercolors, and Drawings from the Collection of Jo Ann and Julian Ganz Jr.* Exh. cat. Santa Barbara: Santa Barbara Museum of Art, 1973. Introduction by Donelson F. Hoopes. Catalogue by Nancy Wall Moure.

———. Hoopes, Donelson. "The Jo Ann and Julian Ganz Collection." *American Art Review* 1, no. 1 (September-October 1973): 48–58.

———. *An American Perspective: Nineteenth-Century Art from the Collection of Jo Ann & Julian Ganz Jr.* Exh. cat. Washington, D.C.: National Gallery of Art, 1981. Essays by John Wilmerding, Linda Ayres, and Earl A. Powell III.

GRANT-MUNGER. *Grant-Munger Collection.* Exh. cat. San Diego: Fine Arts Gallery of San Diego, 1970.

HARRISON. *Catalogue of Paintings by Contemporary American Artists Donated by Mr. and Mrs. William Preston Harrison.* Exh. cat. Los Angeles: Los Angeles Museum of History, Science, and Art, 1918.

———. Harrison, [William] Preston, comp. *A Catalogue of the Mr. and Mrs. William Preston Harrison Galleries of American Art: A Gift to the People.* Los Angeles: Saturday Night Publishing, 1934.

———. *American Pastels & Watercolors: Selections from the Mr. and Mrs. William Preston Harrison Collection.* Exh. cat. Los Angeles: Los Angeles County Museum of Art, 1969. Essay by Larry Curry.

———. Harris, Neil. "William Preston Harrison: The Disappointed Collector." *Archives of American Art Journal* 33, no. 3 (1993): 13–28.

Higgins, Winifred Haines. "Art Collecting in the Los Angeles Area, 1910–1960." Ph.D. dissertation, University of California, Los Angeles, 1963.

HONEYMAN. *Early Prints and Drawings of California from the Robert B. Honeyman Jr. Collection.* Exh. cat. Los Angeles: Los Angeles County Museum of History, Science, and Art, 1954.

———. *Early Paintings of California in the Robert B. Honeyman Jr. Collection.* Exh. cat. Oakland: Oakland Art Museum, 1956.

———. Baird, Joseph Armstrong, Jr., comp. *Catalogue of Original Paintings, Drawings, and Watercolors in the Robert B. Honeyman Jr. Collection.* Berkeley: Friends of the Bancroft Library, University of California, 1968.

Hooper. See Santa Barbara Museum of Art 1967.

Huntington Library and Art Gallery, San Marino, 1984. *The Virginia Steele Scott Gallery: A Gift to the Huntington Art Collection.*

———, 1995. Nygren, Edward J. *In Celebration of Collecting: Selected Works from the Collections of Friends of the Huntington.* Exh. cat.

Hutson, Martha. "Nineteenth Century American Art Collections in Los Angeles," *American Art Review* 2, no. 5 (September-October 1975): 62–78.

Katz. *Masters of American Modernism: Vignettes from the Katz Collection.* Exh. cat. Long Beach: University Art Museum, California State University, 1995. Constance W. Glenn, ed. Essay by Jay Cantor.

Los Angeles County Museum of Art, 1973–93. American Art Council Newsletter. Typescript.

———, 1974. *American Paintings from Los Angeles Collections.* Exh. cat.

Ludington. Seldis, Henry J. "Harmony in Diversity: Wright S. Ludington." In Jean Lipman, comp., *The Collector in America.* New York: Viking Press, 1961.

———. *The Ludington Collection.* Exh. cat. Los Angeles: UCLA Art Galleries, 1964.

Mabury. *The Paul Rodman Mabury Collection of Paintings.* Los Angeles: Los Angeles County Museum of History, Science, and Art, c. 1940. Foreword by Preston Harrison.

Mallory. See Santa Barbara Museum of Art 1966B.

McMurray. *American Painting of the Nineteenth Century: The George F. McMurray Collection.* Exh. cat. Pasadena: Pasadena Art Museum, 1960.

Morton. Mead, Katherine Harper, ed. *The Preston Morton Collection of American Art.* Santa Barbara: Santa Barbara Museum of Art, 1981.

Previn. See Santa Barbara Museum of Art 1967.

Ries. *A Time and Place: From the Ries Collection of California Painting.* Exh. cat. Oakland: Oakland Museum, 1990. Foreword by Michael Quick. Essays by James and Linda Ries and Paul C. Mills.

San Diego Museum of Art, 1981. *Catalogue of American Painting.*

Santa Barbara Museum of Art, 1966A. *American Portraits in California Collections.* Exh. cat.

———, 1966B. *Two Collections: Margaret Mallory—Ala Story.* Exh. cat. Essay by Henry J. Seldis.

———, 1967. *Three Young Collections: Donald and Lynn Factor, Dennis and Brooke Hooper, Andre and Dory Previn.* Exh. cat.

———, 1985. *Santa Barbara Collects.* Exh. cat.

Seldis, Henry J. *Hollywood Collects.* Exh. cat. Los Angeles: Otis Art Institute, 1970.

Story. See Santa Barbara Museum of Art 1966B.

Trevey. Robertson, Bruce. *Representing America: The Ken Trevey Collection of American Realist Prints.* Exh. cat. Santa Barbara: University Art Museum, University of California, 1995.

Walbridge. *The Walbridge Legacy.* Exh. cat. San Diego: San Diego Museum of Art, 1988.

County of Los Angeles

Los Angeles County Museum of Art Board of Trustees, Fiscal Year 1995–96

Honorary Life Trustees

Past Presidents